Cambridge Elements ≡

Elements in Public Economics
edited by
Robin Boadway
Queen's University
Frank A. Cowell
London School of Economics and Political Science
Massimo Florio
University of Milan

THE PUBLIC ECONOMICS OF CHANGING LONGEVITY

Pierre Pestieau
*HEC, University of Liège and
CORE, University of Louvain*

CAMBRIDGE
UNIVERSITY PRESS

University Printing House, Cambridge CB2 8BS, United Kingdom

One Liberty Plaza, 20th Floor, New York, NY 10006, USA

477 Williamstown Road, Port Melbourne, VIC 3207, Australia

314–321, 3rd Floor, Plot 3, Splendor Forum, Jasola District Centre,
New Delhi – 110025, India

103 Penang Road, #05–06/07, Visioncrest Commercial, Singapore 238467

Cambridge University Press is part of the University of Cambridge.

It furthers the University's mission by disseminating knowledge in the pursuit of
education, learning, and research at the highest international levels of excellence.

www.cambridge.org
Information on this title: www.cambridge.org/9781009170857
DOI: 10.1017/9781009170864

© Pierre Pestieau 2022

First published 2022

A catalogue record for this publication is available from the British Library.

ISBN 978-1-009-17085-7 Paperback
ISSN 2516-2276 (online)
ISSN 2516-2268 (print)

The Public Economics of Changing Longevity

Elements in Public Economics

DOI: 10.1017/9781009170864
First published online: January 2022

Pierre Pestieau
HEC, University of Liège and CORE, University of Louvain

Author for correspondence: Pierre Pestieau, p.pestieau@ulg.ac.be

Abstract: Our societies are witnessing a steady increase in longevity. This demographic evolution is accompanied by some convergence across countries, but at the same time substantial longevity inequalities persist within nations across income classes. This Element aims to survey some crucial implications of changing longevity on the design of optimal public policy. For that purpose, it first focuses on some difficulties raised by risky and varying lifetime for the representation of individual and social preferences. Then, it explores some central implications of changing longevity for optimal policy making, regarding prevention of premature death, pension policies, education, health care, and long-term care. The author distinguishes between the case in which longevity is partially the responsibility of individuals and the case in which longevity is plainly exogenous.

Keywords: longevity, optimal public policy, aging, endogenous longevity, life expectancy

JEL classifications: H21, H55, I12, I13, J10

ISBNs: 9781009170857 (PB), 9781009170864 (OC)
ISSNs: 2516-2276 (online), 2516-2268 (print)

Contents

1 Introduction

Globally, people are living longer. Today, for the first time in history, most people have a life expectancy of over sixty years. By 2050, the world population aged sixty and over is expected to reach 2 billion, up from 900 million in 2015. Today, 125 million people are aged eighty and over. By 2050, 80 percent of older people will live in low- and middle-income countries. The aging of the global population is also accelerating sharply. For example, while France has had almost 150 years to adapt to the increase in the share of people aged sixty and over in the population (which has increased from 10 to 20 percent over this period), Brazil, China, and India have had a little over twenty years to do so. Longer life opens up possibilities, not only for older people and their families, but also for society as a whole. These extra years are an opportunity to embark on new activities, for example, further training, a new career, or a long-neglected passion. Seniors also make a wide variety of contributions to their families and communities. However, the magnitude of these opportunities and contributions depends largely on one factor: health. And it cannot be stated clearly enough that older people live their last years in better health than did their parents.

Although over the past thirty years, rates of severe disability have declined in high-income countries, there has been no significant change for mild or moderate disability. If people live those extra years in good health and in a supportive environment, their ability to do what they enjoy will be quite similar to that of young people. If, in contrast, these years are marked by a decrease in physical and mental capacities, the consequences for the elderly and for society will be more negative. Beyond biological changes, aging is also associated with other life transitions such as retirement, relocation to more suitable housing, and the death of friends or partners. Taking public health action in the face of aging requires approaches that not only reduce losses associated with aging, but also enhance recovery, adaptation, and psychosocial development. Old age is characterized by the onset of several complex health conditions that usually do not appear until later in life and do not constitute separate disease categories. These are commonly referred to as geriatric syndromes. All these elements explain why the concept of life expectancy in good health has been developed. As we will see, longevity in good health generally increases but not at the same pace as plain longevity.

The pervasive increase in longevity has lately attracted the attention of economists who are concerned by two facts. First, behind an apparent steady trend, there remains a lot of variability across individuals, or, rather, across groups of individuals segmented according to characteristics such as gender, occupation, location, and education. Hence, heterogeneity in individual characteristics affecting survival chances is a central dimension of the problem at stake. Second, a sizeable part of longevity changes is endogenous, that is, triggered by individual and collective decisions. As a consequence, longevity changes can hardly be treated as exogenous shocks affecting the economy, but, rather, can be better viewed as the output of a complex production process. In this Element, we plan to review some major effects that evolving longevity has on a number of public policies, which were initially designed for unchanged longevity. For that purpose, it is important to start by studying the challenges raised by varying longevity for the description of individual preferences and the social welfare criterion. On that basis, we will be able to analyze a number of questions pertaining to the design of optimal public intervention in the context of varying longevity. The questions are related to the areas of health care, pensions, disability, wealth distribution, education, poverty, and growth. Here is a sample of issues that are treated in this Element:

- Longevity is partially endogenous and this implies some free-riding. How should the state react to this source of inefficiency?
- Given that longevity genes or learning ability are private information, how should public policy be adjusted?
- Longevity increase has an impact on education decisions. Is there a role for the government?
- Longevity increase combined with social security has a definite effect on economic growth. Should the government intervene?
- Longevity changes have an impact on income inequality and poverty particularly given that mortality varies with income. How does that affect redistributive policies?

This Element is organized as follows. Section 2 presents basic definitions and key empirical facts on longevity and life expectancy. Section 3 discusses the challenges raised by unequal longevity for both individual and collective choices. Section 4 presents a number of public policy issues that have to be revisited in the context of risky and unequal lifetimes. It focuses on cases in which longevity is exogenous. Section 5 is concerned with the case of endogenous longevity. Concluding remarks are drawn in Section 6.

This Element draws on our previous work, in particular the surveys of Pestieau and Ponthière (2014a, b). We are grateful to our coauthors and especially Gregory Ponthière who over the years helped us to reflect on the various implications that declining mortality and age- and income-differentiated longevity may have on the design of public policy.

2 Concepts and Figures

2.1 Aging and Dependency

Aging can be understood in two different but related ways. One can indeed distinguish between individual and population aging. Individual aging means the process of one's becoming old or older. Aging is then measured by longevity or by life expectancy. This has been steadily increasing globally, as we show below. Population aging is a shift in the distribution of a country's population towards older ages. It is due to declining fertility and rising longevity. This is usually reflected in an increase in the population's mean and median ages, a decline in the proportion of the population composed of children, and a rise in the proportion of the population composed of the elderly. Population aging is widespread across the world. It is most advanced in the most highly developed countries, but it is now growing more quickly in less developed regions, too.

Population aging is traditionally measured by dependency ratios. The best-known dependency ratio is the age-population ratio, namely, the ratio of those typically not in the labor force (the dependent part, those aged 0 to fourteen and those over sixty-five) and those typically in the labor force (the productive part, those aged fifteen to sixty-four). It is used to measure the pressure on the productive population. One can also use the old age dependency ratio, that is, the ratio of those aged over sixty-five to those aged fifteen to sixty-four. This ratio is convenient to study the sustainability of social security and health care systems. In OECD member countries, the old age dependency ratio has increased from 13 to 26 percent over the past six decades. As appears from Table 1, in the OECD, Japan has the highest ratio and Mexico the lowest. As a widely accepted

Table 1 Old age dependency ratios in some OECD countries, 2020

Countries	Old age dependency ratio
France	33
Germany	33
Italy	36
Japan	47
Mexico	11
UK	29
USA	25

Source: OECD (2020)

convention, the threshold age for measuring dependency is sixty-five. If we consider that people may become healthier over time, this threshold should be adjusted upward, which would result in a less sharp increase in dependency.

2.2 Life Expectancy

Life expectancy is a statistical measure of the average time someone is expected to live for, based on the year of their birth, current age, and other demographic factors including their sex. It is used to assess and set a number of important policies that impact on everyday life, for example, setting retirement age and targeting health policy initiatives. To calculate life expectancy, one uses a life table that shows, for each age, what the probability is that a person will die before their next birthday. There are two different types of life table: cohort and period.

A cohort life table shows the probability of a person from a given cohort dying at each age over the course of lifetime. In this context, a cohort refers to a group of people with the same year of birth. The cohort life table is based on age-specific probabilities of death, which are calculated using observed mortality data from the cohort. A cohort life table takes into account observed and projected improvements in mortality for the cohort throughout its lifetime. Cohort figures are therefore regarded as the appropriate measure of how long a person of a given age would be expected to live on average.

An alternative way of looking at life expectancies is the use of period life expectancies, rather than cohort life expectancies. Period life expectancies use mortality rates from a single year (or group of years) and assume that those rates apply throughout the remainder of a person's life. This means that any future changes to mortality rates would not be taken into account. Period life expectancies are the traditional measure of mortality rates in international comparisons. Needless to say, period life expectancies tend to be lower than cohort life expectancies because they do not include any assumptions about future improvements in mortality rates. In other words, *published* life expectancies tend to understate *actual* longevity.

Let us look at some stylized facts on the evolution of human longevity. For that purpose, a natural starting point consists of considering the evolution of period life expectancy at birth during the last few centuries. As shown in Figure 1, period life expectancy at birth has grown strongly during the last three centuries. Whereas life expectancy was equal to about thirty-eight years in 1750 in Sweden, it is nowadays over eighty-two years. Figure 1 shows also that the extent of growth in life expectancy has not been constant over time: life expectancy growth was particularly strong in the first part of the twentieth century,

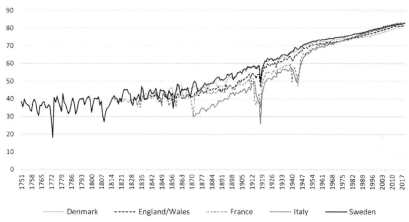

Figure 1 Life expectancy at birth (period) in several European countries, 1750–2019

Source: Human Mortality Database (2012)

but less so ince then. Another important thing that appears in Figure 1 is the convergence between countries: whereas significant inequalities existed in terms of life expectancy in the early twentieth century, those inequalities are, one century later, much smaller. The life expectancies of Italy and Sweden in 1875 were respectively equal to 33.78 and 46.20; in 2015, they were 82.82 and 82.51.

When interpreting Figure 1, it is important to bear in mind that each point represents the expected duration of life conditional on the survival likelihood prevailing during that year. This explains why period life expectancy data vary strongly at the time of the First World War and the Second World War. Another key feature of periodic data lies in the fact that those life expectancies only predict the effective average duration of life provided age-specific probabilities of death remain constant over time. In light of this, it may well be the case that the large period life expectancy levels measured in the early twenty-first century underestimate the average duration of life for the people born in the early twenty-first century.

In order to give an idea of potential bias, let us compare, for the eighteenth and nineteenth centuries, the period life expectancy at birth with the cohort life expectancy at birth, that is, the average effective duration of life among a group of people born at the same point in time. As shown in Figure 2 for Sweden, the gap between the period and the cohort life expectancies at birth remained relatively small during the eighteenth century, but, after that, the cohort life expectancy remained permanently above the period life expectancy. The gap between, on the one hand, the duration of life that could be expected on

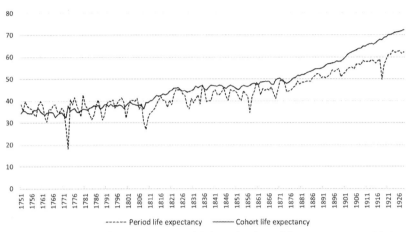

Figure 2 Period life expectancy at birth and cohort life expectancy at birth,
Sweden, 1751–1928

Source: Human Mortality Database (2012)

the basis of observed age-specific probabilities of death, and, on the other hand, the average realized duration of life, is growing over time. In 1751, cohort and period life expectancy were respectively equal to 34.81 and 37.72, whereas, in 1928, they were equal to 71.78 and 62.25. This suggests that the accuracy of period life expectancy figures as proxies for actual average durations of life – which is perfect in periods of stationary survival conditions – should not be overestimated. Actually, the observed trend in period life expectancy gives us a qualitative clue regarding the future patterns of the average duration of life, rather than an exact magnitude of the lengthening of life that will take place in the twenty-first century.

2.3 Survival Curves and Rectangularization

In addition to the use of life expectancy statistics, another way to measure the fall of mortality consists of using survival curves. Period survival curves give us the proportion of a cohort that reaches each age of life, conditional on the age-specific probabilities of death prevailing during that year. Such a focus on the probabilities to reach the different ages of life allows us to go beyond the mere analysis of the average duration of life.

As shown in Figure 3 with the example of England and Wales, survival curves have moved substantially during the last two centuries. Two distinct movements have taken place. First, survival curves tended to shift upwards, implying that an increasingly large proportion of the population can reach a high age. This movement is known as the rectangularization of the survival

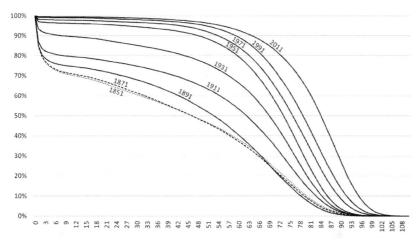

Figure 3 Survival curves (period), total population, England and Wales (1851–2011)

Source: OurWorldinData.org

curve. In the hypothetical case of a perfectly rectangular survival curve, there would be no risk about the duration of life, since all individuals would die at the same age.

Accordingly, in that hypothetical case, there would be no inequality in terms of realized longevity. The second movement of the survival curve consists of a shift to the right, implying that the duration of life lived by the long-lived is increasing over time. This second movement can be regarded as a kind of increase in the limit longevity. That second movement has also been at work in the last few centuries. Note that this shift to the right is distinct from the shift upwards, since this does not necessarily imply a reduction in longevity risk. Although the two movements have been at work during the last two centuries, the rectangularization has been the dominant movement during the nineteenth century, and during the largest part of the twentieth century, whereas the rise in the limit longevity has been dominant in the last thirty years.

One important thing that we learn from Figure 3 concerns the size and extent of longevity inequalities. The survival curves for 1851–1911 show that child mortality was a widespread phenomenon in those times, whose size has strongly decreased during the twentieth century. But even if we concentrate on the survival curves for 1951–2011, we see that the proportion of individuals reaching, let us say, the age of sixty has reatgly increased. That decreasing trend in inequality is unambiguously good news. Note, however, that those figures can be interpreted in a less optimistic way. The 2011 survival curve tells us that, on the basis of the survival conditions prevailing in 2011, there is still

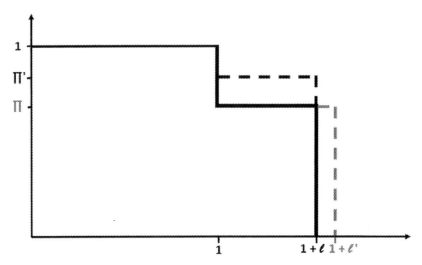

Figure 4 Survival curve in a two-period model

a not negligible proportion of individuals who will be dead before reaching the age of sixty, suggesting that longevity inequalities remain substantial even now.

In the following sections, we will use a simple representation of the survival curve. The setting we adopt is one of a two-period life cycle. The first (active) period has a unitary length and the second (retirement) period has a length of $l < 1$. This second period is uncertain with a survival probability π. In such a setting life expectancy is equal to $1 + \pi l$. Life expectancy can be increased through an increase of either the lifetime horizon $1 + l$ or the survival probability π. An increase in π leads to a more rectangular survival curve. Rectangularization would be complete with $\pi = 1$. In Figure 4, the increase in l and that in π lead to the same longevity but to a different shape of the survival curve. In other words: $1 + \pi l' = 1 + \pi' l$.

2.4 Longevity Differentials Across Individuals

Although longevity disparities across countries have been falling over time, there remain, nonetheless, significant longevity differentials across individuals. Longevity differs across persons because of differences in a range of characteristics, including gender, ethnicity, and educational background. To illustrate this, let us first look at the evolution of life expectancy at birth for males and females in Sweden. As shown in Figure 5, over the three centuries under consideration, women exhibited a higher life expectancy than did men. The gender

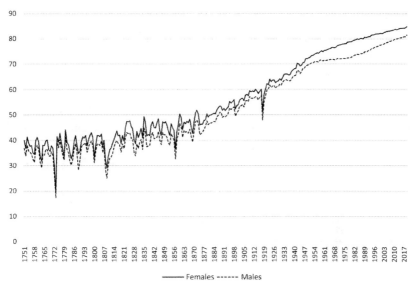

Figure 5 Life expectancy at birth (period) for females and males, Sweden
(1751–2019)

Source: Human Mortality Database (2012)

gap increased between 1950 and 1980. Then it decreased during the last thirty
years. It was equal to six years in 1980 and dropped below four years in 2019.

Besides gender, another important characteristic that is correlated with longevity inequalities is ethnicity. This point was highlighted by Sen (1998),
who argued that the life expectancy of black males in poor US neighborhoods
was in some cases lower than the one prevailing in developing countries. A
recent study by Arias (2014) shows that, for the USA, the white/black gap in
life expectancy at birth is equal to 3.5 years for women and to 5.3 years for
men. When considering life expectancy at age sixty-five, longevity differentials remain, although their sizes are smaller. Black females' life expectancy at
age sixty-five remains one year smaller than that of white females, whereas for
males the gap is about two years.

Another important source of longevity inequality lies in educational background. In a study using US data, Hendi (2017) shows that among non-Hispanic
whites, the life expectancy at age twenty-five was, in 2009, twelve years lower
for men with low educational background than for men with a bachelor's
degree. For females, the education gap is barely smaller: it is equal to 11.7 years.
Among non-Hispanic blacks, these gaps are even larger. They are, respectively, equal to 13 and 12.5 years. Education-based inequalities in longevity
are growing over time. Life expectancy at age twenty-five has increased quite

significantly for highly educated men and women between 1990 and 2009, while it has remained almost stable for low educated men and women with the exception of non-Hispanic black men.

Combining education and ethnicity has led to some somewhat surprising findings over the last decade. Case and Deaton (2020) observe marked differences in mortality by race and education, with mortality among white non-Hispanics (males and females) rising for those without a college degree, and falling for those with a college degree. In contrast, mortality rates among blacks and Hispanics have continued to fall, irrespective of educational attainment.

In sum, these few figures illustrate that, inspite of a substantial improvement in survival conditions on average, there remain significant inequalities in longevity achievements. Those demographic facts raise deep challenges to policy-makers: how can public policy adapt to the increase in average longevity, while providing more redistribution towards those unlucky short-lived people?

2.5 Healthy Life Expectancy

Life expectancy at birth is still increasing in most countries, thanks mainly to lower mortality at advanced ages. But are the years gained spent in good health, or with disabilities and in a state of dependence? This question is important not only for the organization of healthcare and long-term care services, but also for social and economic reasons: raising the retirement age unless those concerned are healthy and self-sufficient is questionable. Estimating the number of healthy years that people can expect to live for provides crucial information for policy-makers. In 2004–5, life expectancy without activity limitation was added to the European Union's list of social indicators.

The European Union Statistics on Income and Living Conditions surveys, coordinated by Eurostat, collect health data on the populations of European Union countries via three questions that concern "perceived health," "chronic morbidity," and "activity limitations." Those three types of health expectancy are obtained by matching the frequencies of persons reporting health problems against the life table. Of course, these data are partially driven by the respondents' subjectivity and health may be perceived differently from one country to another; this is an other important factor to be considered in studies of this kind.

Table 2 provides some data for healthy and gross life expectancy for a number of countries. While European women have a much longer life expectancy than men, their healthy life expectancy is very similar. One exception is Iceland where healthy life expectancy of women is lower than that of men.

Table 2 Life expectancy and healthy life expectancy, 2018

Countries	Men		Women	
	Healthy LE	Gross LE	Healthy LE	Gross LE
France	63.4	79.7	65.5	85.9
Germany	65.1	78.6	66.9	83.3
UK	61.5	79.5	60.8	83.1
Iceland	69.6	81.3	63.7	84.5
Poland	60.5	73.7	64.3	81.7

Source: Eurostat (2020)

2.6 Centenarians

How do we define the "oldest" old people and what is old age? Old age has a number of different conceptualizations. It can be defined as the last stage of an individual's life, although we often only know that in retrospect. More usually we use a specific chronological age for policy and practice reasons to define eligibilities for benefits such as pensions at one end or to determine entitlements such as voting at the other. We also use specific ages to define specific segments of our population such as teenagers or older people. The use of a specific age to define old age is highly arbitrary. A century ago, old age was defined as "any age after fifty." The fraction of people above fifty was then the same as that of nonagenerians today. Conventionally, however, most developed countries use the age of sixty or over sixty-five to define the older population for demographic purposes. While there is some consensus internationally in the use of specific ages to define old age from a demographic or policy perspective, there is no such agreement as to the chronological age at which individuals become "old." To illustrate the emergence of significant numbers of centenarians here is an anecdote. In 1917, the king of England, George V, sent out the first congratulatory letter to those who had reached their 100th birthday. There were then thirty-five of them. In 1990, British centenarians numbered 4,062, last year 15,834 and in 2050, there will likely be some 55,000.[1] In 2020, the United Nations expected the number of centenarians to rise to 573,423 worldwide. In 1960, it was 20,119. In sixty years, it has thus multiplied by about twenty-nine. The US has the highest absolute number of centenarians in the world with 97,000 living in the country. Japan comes second with 79,000 Japanese who are over one hundred years old. Japan is also the country in which the world's

---

[1] Teixeira et al. (2020).

oldest person lives. Kane Tanaka from the Fukuoka prefecture is 118 years old, making her a so-called supercentenarian, which is a person living to or beyond the age of 110. It is estimated that there are between 150 and 600 living people who have reached the age of 110. The true number is uncertain as not all super-centenarians are known to researchers at a given time and some claims either cannot be validated or are fraudulent.[2]

The increase in the number of centenarians and supercentenarians seems to imply a trend towards the derectangularization of the survival curves, which has consequences on the design of public policies. Let us recall that such a trend would imply that the variability in the age at death increases and that the compression of deaths into the upper years of life declines.

2.7 Retirement and Dependency

The threshold age used to measure the ratio of dependency of a country is sixty-five, which is quite often the usual age for receiving a full old age pension. A more appropriate indicator of dependency could be the average effective age at which older workers withdraw from the labor force, which is usually referred to as the effective age of retirement. In almost all OECD countries, the effective retirement age has declined substantially since 1970. But this trend decline has been interrupted recently. Over the past two decades, most countries have experienced either a flattening out of the trend or a small upturn (see Table 3). But even in Japan, the effective retirement age remains below the levels of the 1970s.

It is clear that if we were to use these ages instead of sixty-five, we would end up with a different profile of the ratio of dependency: much lower for Japan and quite significantly higher for France. The evolution of that ratio would also

Table 3 Average effective age of retirement in some OECD countries, men, 1970–2018

Countries	1970	1990	2000	2018
USA	68.4	64.7	64.8	67.9
UK	67.7	62.8	62.5	64.7
Germany	66.5	62.2	61.0	64.0
France	67.9	60.4	59.0	60.8
Japan	72.8	70.6	70.1	70.8

Source: OECD (2020)

---

[2] Newman (2019).

be different. In France, life expectancy of men increased from 68.4 to 79.6 over the period 1970–2018; at the same time, effective retirement declined from 67.9 to 60.8.

2.8 Replacement Migration

Fertility is below replacement level in all European countries, and population growth is expected to decline in the coming decades. Increasing life expectancy will accentuate concomitant aging of the population. Migration has been seen as a possible means to decelerate aging. In an influential study, the United Nations (2001) addressed the question of whether replacement migration is a solution to declining and aging populations. Replacement migration refers to the international migration that would be needed to offset declines in the size of population and declines in the population of working age, as well as to offset the overall ageing of a population.

The UN study was motivated by the implicit underlying assumption that population decline and increases in the old age dependency ratio have negative consequences that should be avoided. The study illustrated under which hypothetical future migration patterns these consequences could be avoided. A number of realistic scenarios were analyzed. The main conclusion was that the levels of migration needed to offset population aging (i.e., maintain potential support ratios) are extremely high, and, in all cases, entail vastly more immigration than has occurred in the past.

Recently, several studies (see Lutz et al. (2019), Marois et al. (2020)) attempt to update the UN study. They all conclude that sustainable migration cannot be the solution to aging, but that raising labor force participation (particularly for women) and improved education of natives and migrants have the power to nullify aging-related worries. One of the major findings of these studies is that high volumes of immigration would increase labor force size, but would have a very limited impact on the dependency ratio. Higher volumes of immigration would increase not only the working population but also the population of non-workers too as immigrants inevitably age, leave the labor force, and require social assistance, as do native-born workers. That said, in this Element, we do not deal with such migration issues.

2.9 Life Expectancy, Economic Growth, and Environmental Quality

Finally, let us mention two stylized facts that will be used in Section 5. There is first the cross-sectional evidence of a positive relation between life expectancy and economic growth and that between environmental quality and longevity.

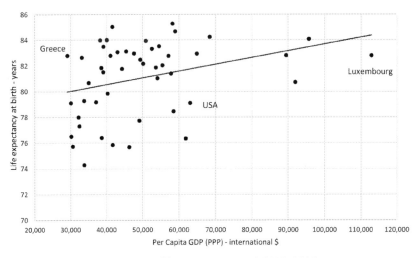

Figure 6 Life expectancy and GDP, 2020

Source: Statistics Times and Worldometers

Not only specific medical innovations, such as vaccinations or antibiotics, were necessary, but also public health interventions – improved public sanitation and publicly funded healthcare – were crucial in dealing with all the many causes of death, from infectious diseases including smallpox and malaria to noncommunicable diseases such as cancer. Given that health spending is closely linked to income, it is not surprising to find an association between income growth and increasing life expectancy both at the level of the individual and that of nations. This being said there are other factors of good health including life style. In the association between GDP and life expectancy we saw in Figure 6, the USA is an outlier. It achieves only a comparatively short life expectancy considering the fact that the country has by far the highest health expenditure of any country in the world.

The environment directly affects health status and plays a major role in quality of life, years of healthy life lived, and health disparities. Poor air quality is linked to premature death, cancer, and long-term damage to respiratory and cardiovascular systems. Secondhand smoke containing toxic and cancer-causing chemicals contributes to heart disease and lung cancer in nonsmoking adults. Globally, a large chunk of all deaths and the total disease burden can be attributed to environmental factors. Figure 7 provides the cross-country relation between environmental quality, measure by EPI, and life expectancy.

We will come back to those stylized associations. As we shall see, they have to be taken with caution and should not be seen as signaling any kind of causality one way or the other.

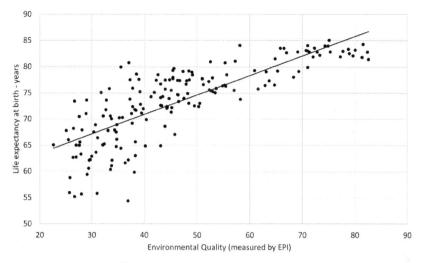

Figure 7 Life expectancy and environmental quality, 2020

Source: Wendling et al. (2020)

3 Individual Choice and Social Valuation

3.1 Individual Choice

In order to examine the challenges raised by longevity variations, it is necessary to consider how the variation of survival conditions is taken into account in the standard economic model of the life cycle, which is used as a benchmark for studying decisions such as savings, retirement, education, and prevention. For that purpose, we develop a two-period life cycle model with risky lifetime, where all individuals live period 1 (i.e., the young age), but only a proportion $0 < \pi < 1$ of the cohort enjoys period 2 (i.e., the old age), whose duration is equal to $0 < l \le 1$). This discrete time framework constitutes a simplified model, which makes the representation of life-cycle decisions simpler by reducing life to two periods: the young age and the old age. We discuss, within that model, how the representation of individual preferences reflects their attitude towards mortality risks. Then, we will focus on the existence of horizon effects in various economic decisions. Following that, we will consider the endogeneity of survival conditions.

3.1.1 Attitudes Towards Mortality Risk

In the standard life-cycle model, individual preferences over consumption profiles are represented by a weighted sum of temporal utility functions, where the weights represent individual time preferences. In a two-period case (young age, old age), this yields the following representation:

$$U(c, d) = u(c) + \beta l u(d)$$

where c denotes first-period and d denotes second-period consumption, while β is a time preference parameter $(0 < \beta \leq 1)$ and l is the maximum duration of the second period. The temporal utility function is usually supposed to be increasing and concave in consumption. Let us now introduce some risk regarding the duration of life, and suppose that the probability of survival to old age is equal to $0 < \pi < 1$. Assuming that individuals die either at the beginning of the second period or at time $1 + l$, life expectancy at birth is equal to

$$1 + \pi l.$$

Once the risk about the duration of life is introduced, preferences are now defined on lotteries of life, specifying a particular duration of life and its probability of occurrence. If one adopts the standard expected utility hypothesis, preferences on lotteries of life can be represented as follows:

$$EU(c, d) = \pi[u(c) + \beta l u(d)] + (1 - \pi)u(c) = u(c) + \beta\pi l u(d)$$

where the temporal utility associated to death is normalized to 0. Note that, in this representation, the survival probability plays a similar role to the one of the pure discount factor β. This explains why π is often regarded as a natural or biological discount factor. As stressed by Bommier (2006, 2007, 2010), an interesting feature of this representation of individual preferences lies in the implicit postulate of net risk neutrality with respect to the duration of life. Net risk neutrality with respect to the duration of life is defined as follows. An individual exhibits net risk neutrality with respect to the duration of his life if, provided there is no pure time preference $(\beta = 1)$ and provided consumption profiles are flat $(c = d)$, he is strictly indifferent between lotteries of life that yield the same expected duration of life, independently of how risky those lotteries are. In a two-period case, net risk neutrality about the duration of life implies, for instance, the strict indifference between the following two lotteries: lottery 1, where $c = d = \hat{c}, \pi = 1$ and $l = 1/2$, and lottery 2, where $c = d = \hat{c}, \pi = 1/2$ and $l = 1$. These two lotteries exhibit the same life expectancy, but differ quite significantly: whereas lottery 1 is degenerate, and guarantees a life of duration 1.5 for sure, lottery 2 is far more risky, and involves two equally likely scenarios, where the duration of life equals 1 and 2 respectively. The standard representation of individual preferences over lotteries of life shown above leads to the same kind of indifference. However, as Bommier pointed out, this kind of indifference is unlikely in real life. Hence Bommier proposed to modify the standard model of the life cycle, by relaxing the assumption of additive lifetime welfare. When lifetime well-being becomes a concave transform of the sum of temporal welfare:

$$U(c, d) = \phi[u(c) + \beta l u(d)]$$

with $\phi'(.) > 0$ and $\phi''(.) < 0$, the expected lifetime well-being becomes:

$$EU(c, d) = \pi\phi[u(c) + \beta lu(d)] + (1 - \pi)\phi[u(c)].$$

When preferences are represented by that function, individuals are no longer risk neutral with respect to the duration of their life. It is easy to see that they are risk averse due to the concavity of $\phi(.)$. To illustrate this, let us turn back to our example. The expected lifetime well-being of lottery 1 is equal to $\phi[1.5u(\hat{c})]$, whereas the one of lottery 2 is equal to $0.5\phi[2u(\hat{c})] + 0.5\phi[u(\hat{c})]$. Given the concavity of $\phi(.)$, the expected lifetime well-being associated to lottery 1 now exceeds the one of lottery 2, implying that net risk neutrality with respect to the duration of life no longer holds. Bommier's critique of the life-cycle model raises an important challenge. Indeed, economists since at least Bernoulli (1730) consider that risk aversion with respect to money is an important feature of human behavior, which deserves to be taken into account in their analyses. However, before Bommier's work, there was little emphasis on individual attitude towards a major risk in life: the risk of death. But, at the same time, Bommier's formulation raises the complexity of the study of the life cycle, which is a new challenge for economists.

3.1.2 Horizon Effects

Having discussed how the attitude towards risk with respect to the duration of life affects the representation of individual preferences on lotteries of life, let us now consider some implications of this for economic decisions. A first decision to be considered is the savings decision, which has been studied in detail by economists since Yaari (1965). It is intuitive to expect that, as survival conditions improve, individuals would rationally choose to save more. However, things may not be as simple as expected at first glance. In order to examine the impact of survival conditions on savings, let us assume that there exists a perfect annuity market with actuarially fair return, so that the interest factor for savings is equal to $\widetilde{R} = R/\pi$. Let us assume also that the individual works during the entire young age and receives a wage w, and that he retires at the beginning of the old age. The savings problem is:

$$max_s \pi\phi\left[u(u - s) + \beta lu(\frac{Rs}{\pi l})\right] + (1 - \pi)\phi[u(w - s)].$$

The first-order condition for optimal savings is:

$$\pi\phi'\left[u(w - s) + \beta lu(\frac{Rs}{\pi l})\right]\left[u'(u - s) + \beta u'(\frac{Rs}{\pi l})\frac{R}{\pi}\right]$$
$$= (1 - \pi)\phi'[u(w - s)]u'(w - s). \tag{1}$$

Obviously, if individuals are risk neutral with respect to the duration of life, we have $\phi'(.)$ equal to a constant. Hence the optimal saving condition reduces to:

$$u'(w-s) = \beta Ru'(\frac{Rs}{\pi l}).$$

We observe that a rise in π and a rise in l have a symmetric effect on optimal saving. Both tend to raise the optimal amount of savings ceteris paribus. Indeed, when either π or l increases, this reduces the level of old age consumption for a given amount of saving, which raises the marginal utility of old age consumption, inviting a rise in savings. Under risk neutrality with respect to the duration of life, the source of the increase in life expectancy – i.e., π or l – does not matter; only the fact that life expectancy grows matters.

However, those two sources of life expectancy gain are no longer equivalent once risk aversion with respect to the length of life is introduced. To see this, note first that a rise in the duration of the old age l does not affect the RHS of the FOC, but this reduces the first factor of the LHS (assuming $u(\frac{Rs}{\pi l})$ − $\frac{Rs}{\pi l}u'(\frac{Rs}{\pi l}) > 0$.) and raises the second factor of the LHS. The impact of a rise in the duration of the old age on savings is thus ambiguous, unlike in the baseline model. The effect of a rise in π is more complex. A rise in π raises the first factor of the LHS, but has an ambiguous effect on the second factor of the RHS, and reduces the LHS. Thus the impact of a rise in π is also ambiguous. To assess the implications of risk aversion with respect to the duration of life on optimal savings, let us rewrite the FOC (1) as:

$$u'(w-s) = \beta u'(\frac{Rs}{\pi l})\frac{R}{\pi} - \frac{(1-\pi)\phi'\left[u(w-s)\right]u'(w-s)}{\pi\phi'\left[u(w-s) + \beta lu(\frac{Rs}{\pi l})\right]}.$$

Obviously, when $\pi = 1$, we have $u'(w-s) = Ru'(\frac{Rs}{l})$, and the optimal savings is the same as under risk neutrality. However, once $\pi < 1$, the LHS of this condition remains the same as in the benchmark case, but the first term of the RHS is now raised, pushing towards more savings in comparison to the baseline case, whereas the second term is negative, pushing towards fewer savings. If $\phi(.)$ is strongly concave, we have $\phi'\left[u(w-s)\right] \gg \phi'\left[u(w-s) + \beta lu\left(\frac{Rs}{\pi l}\right)\right]$, which would push towards less savings. Thus the introduction of risk aversion may lead, in theory, to either larger or smaller savings, the latter case being more plausible when individuals are strongly risk averse.

Regarding the impact of the lifetime horizon l, note that a rise in l raises the first term of the RHS, leading to more savings, as in the benchmark case, but, provided $u\left(\frac{Rs}{\pi l}\right) - \frac{Rs}{\pi l}u'\left(\frac{Rs}{\pi l}\right) > 0$, this tends also to raise the absolute value of the second term, which is negative, and which pushes towards fewer savings. Hence, in comparison to the risk-neutrality case, a rise in l no longer has the same – unambiguous – impact on savings. It may be the case that a rise in *l* reduces the amount saved, unlike under risk neutrality.

Let us further illustrate the impact of introducing risk aversion with respect to the duration of life by considering education choices. In a seminal contribution, Ben-Porath (1967) argued that the life horizon faced by individuals tends, by raising the welfare gains from educational investments, to push towards larger investments in education. This so-called "Ben-Porath effect" has become, in the recent years, a major mechanism present in models of long-run economic dynamics (see de la Croix & Licandro, 2013).

To show how risk aversion affects education choices, let us consider a framework in which individuals, who can work in the two periods, decide to spend a fraction *e* of the young age for education ($0 < e < 1$), and receive, in the second period, a return on education under the form of a wage premium $h(e)$, (with $h'(e) > 0, h"(e) < 0$). Assuming no savings, the individual's problem is:

$$max_e \pi \phi \left[u(w(1-e)) + \beta lu(\frac{h(e)w}{l}) \right] + (1-\pi)\phi[u(w(1-e))]$$

The first-order condition for optimal education is:

$$\pi \phi' \left[u(w(1-e)) + \beta lu(\frac{h(e)w}{l}) \right] \left[-u'(w(1-e))w + \beta u'(\frac{h(e)w}{l})h'(e)w \right]$$
$$= (1-\pi)\phi'[u(w(1-e))] \left[wu'(w(1-e)) \right]. \quad (2)$$

Under risk neutrality with respect to longevity, this condition is:

$$u'(w(1-e)) = \pi \beta u'(\frac{h(e)w}{l})h'(e) \quad (3)$$

That condition equalizes, at the margin, the welfare loss due to education (LHS) and the welfare gain from education (RHS). Obviously, a rise in π raises the marginal welfare gain from education, leading to a rise in *e*. Similarly, a rise in *l* raises the marginal welfare gain from education, pushing towards more education. Thus, under risk neutrality with respect to the length of life, an improvement of survival conditions does necessarily imply more education. Once risk aversion with respect to the duration of life is introduced, the condition for optimal education can be written as:

$$u'(w(1-e)) = \beta u'(\frac{h(e)w}{l})h'(e) - \frac{(1-\pi)\phi' \left[u(w(1-e)) \right] u'(w(1-e))}{\pi \phi' \left[u(w(1-e)) + \beta lu \left(\frac{h(e)w}{l} \right) \right]}$$

Obviously, under certain lifetime (i.e., $\pi = 1$), this condition would be the same as under risk neutrality, leading to the same level of education. However, under $\pi < 1$, the LHS remains the same, but the first term of the RHS is not multiplied by π (as in (3) which pushes towards more education, while the additional second term of the RHS is unambiguously negative, and pushing towards less education. Regarding the impact of the lifetime horizon l, note that a rise in l raises the first term of the RHS, leading to more education, as in the benchmark case, but, provided $u\left(\frac{h(e)w}{l}\right) - \frac{h(e)w}{l}u'\left(\frac{h(e)w}{l}\right) > 0$, this tends also to raise the absolute value of the second term, which is negative, and which pushes towards less education. Hence, in comparison to the risk-neutrality case, a rise in l does not have a clear impact on education. It may be the case that a rise in l reduces education, unlike under risk neutrality.

Finally, let us conclude our study of horizon effects by focusing on the retirement decision. For that purpose, let us suppose that individuals can decide the fraction z of the old age that they work ($0 < z < l$). They face some disutility of old age labor $v(z)$, which is increasing and convex. The choice of savings and retirement can be written as:

$$\max_{s,z} \pi\phi\left[u(w-s) + \beta lu\left(\frac{zw}{l} + \frac{Rs}{\pi l}\right) - \beta v(z)\right] + (1-\pi)\phi\left[u(w-s)\right]$$

The first-order condition for optimal savings is now:

$$\pi\phi'\left[u(w-s) + \beta lu\left(\frac{zw}{l} + \frac{Rs}{\pi l}\right) - \beta v(z)\right]$$
$$\times \left[-u'(w-s) + \beta u'\left(\frac{zw}{l} + \frac{Rs}{\pi l}\right)\frac{R}{\pi}\right]$$
$$= (1-\pi)\phi'\left[u(w-s)\right]u'(w-s).$$

The first-order condition for optimal retirement is:

$$\pi\phi'\left[u(w-s) + \beta lu\left(\frac{zw}{l} + \frac{Rs}{\pi l}\right) - \beta v(z)\right]\left[\beta u'\left(\frac{zw}{l} + \frac{Rs}{\pi l}\right)w - \beta v'(z)\right]$$
$$= 0.$$

The condition for optimal retirement can hold only if:

$$u'\left(\frac{zw}{l} + \frac{Rs}{l\pi}\right)w = v'(z)$$

that is, provided the marginal utility of further work at an older age is equal to the marginal utility loss from further old age work. This condition characterizes the optimal retirement age whatever the individual is risk neutral or risk averse with respect to the duration of their life. However, although the condition is formally similar in both cases, the level of the optimal retirement age differs depending on the degree of risk, since this affects, as we have shown, the amount of savings, which influences the marginal welfare gain from old age labour. Clearly, if the individual is more risk averse with respect to longevity, they are likely, as we have shown, to save less, which will push towards more labour at an older age, and, hence, towards the postponement of retirement.

3.1.3 Endogenous Mortality Risks

Up to now, we have considered an economy in which survival probabilities are exogenous to individuals. This constitutes a significant simplification, since humans do, through their behavior, affect their survival chances. Actually, whereas exogenous factors, such as the genetic background, account for a significant part of longevity inequalities (about 30 percent according to Christensen et al. 2006), human behaviors, such as eating, drinking, physical activity, smoking, and sleep patterns, are responsible for about 25 percent of longevity inequalities (see Cotoyannis & Jones, 2004; Balia & Jones, 2008). Among those behavioral factors, one can distinguish between inputs that contribute positively to health production (i.e., prevention, such as physical activity or diet) and inputs that contribute negatively (i.e., "sin" goods, such as tobacco, alcohol, and fatty food).

In order to illustrate the impact of risk aversion with respect to the duration of life on preventive behavior, let us consider the problem faced by an individual who can invest an amount H at a younger age, which reduces his consumption and well-being at that age, but increases the probability of reaching old age, which is now a function $\pi(H)$ that is increasing and concave. In the following, we suppose that there exists a perfect annuity market, and that individuals take into account the impact of prevention on the returns from savings.

Assuming that all individuals retire at the end of the young age, the problem of the choice of optimal prevention can be written as:

$$max_{s,H}\pi(H)\phi\left[u(w - s - H) + \beta lu(d)\right] + (1 - \pi(H))\phi[u(w - s - H)$$

where $d = \frac{Rs}{\pi(H)l}$.

The first-order condition for optimal savings is:

$$\pi(H)\phi'\left[u(w - s - H) + \beta lu(d)\right]\left[-u'(w - s - H) + \beta lu'(d)d\right]$$
$$= (1 - \pi(H))\phi'[u(w\text{-}s\text{-}H)]u'(w\text{-}s\text{-}H)$$

The first-order condition for optimal prevention is:

$$\pi'(H)\phi\left[u(w - s - H) + \beta lu(d)\right]$$
$$+ \pi(H)\phi'\left[u(w - s - H) + \beta lu(d)\right]\left[-u'(w - s - H) + \beta u'(d)\frac{Rs\pi'(H)}{[\pi(H)]^2}\right]$$
$$= \pi'(H)\phi\left[u(w - s - H)\right] + (1 - \pi(H)\phi'\left[u(w - s - H)\right]u'(w - s - H).$$

Under risk neutrality, the FOC for optimal prevention can be reduced to:

$$\pi'(H)\beta\left[lu(d) - u'(d)d\right] = u'(w - s - H).$$

The first term in brackets captures the pure welfare gain from increasing the survival probability, for a given level of old age consumption, whereas the second term in brackets captures the welfare loss due to old age consumption reduction when survival conditions improve. In general, the first term dominates the second one. Given that, from the FOC for savings, we have:

$$u'(w - s - H) = \beta R u'(d),$$

the condition for optimal H can be written as:

$$\pi'(H) l u(d) = u'(d) R \left(1 + \frac{\pi'(H)s}{\pi(H)} \right).$$

A rise in l raises, in general, the LHS of that condition. But it also raises the RHS, so that it is difficult to draw a general conclusion regarding the impact of l on optimal prevention. The reason is that an increase in the duration of old age tends, at the same time, to make survival to old age more worthwhile, but, also, puts some additional pressure on available resources, which discourages spending on prevention. Whether prevention increases or not when l increases depends on which effect dominates the other. Note that things are even more complex when the individual exhibits risk aversion with respect to the duration of life. Substituting for the FOC for optimal savings in the FOC for prevention then yields:

$$\pi'(H) \{ \phi [u(w - s - H) + \beta l u(d)] - \phi[u(w - s - H)] \}$$
$$= \phi' [u(w - s - H) + \beta l u(d)] \left[\beta u'(d) R \left(1 + \frac{\pi'(H)s}{\pi(H)} \right) \right].$$

The LHS of that expression reflects the pure marginal welfare gain from increasing the survival chance to old age, ceteris paribus. Note that, the more concave $\phi(.)$ is, the lower the LHS will be, since, in that case, the gains, in terms of lifetime well-being, from being in an older age bracket are more limited. Thus a higher degree of risk aversion reduces the support for investing in prevention. The RHS captures the marginal welfare loss from increasing prevention. The RHS is close to the one under risk neutrality, except that $u'(d) R \left(1 + \frac{\pi'(H)s}{\pi(H)} \right)$ is now multiplied by $\beta \phi' [u(w - s - H) + \beta l u(d)]$.

Regarding the impact of a rise in the life horizon l, things are more complex than in the benchmark case. But it is likely that the impact of a variation in l on the LHS will be smaller than under risk neutrality, whereas a rise in l is likely also to reduce the first factor of the RHS. The effect is thus quite ambiguous. Obviously, more precise assumptions on the functions $\phi(.), u(.)$ and $\pi(.)$ are required in order to be able to draw more accurate conclusions regarding the existence of horizon effects for prevention decisions.

3.2 Normative Foundations

The extension of longevity requires not only a careful modeling of the life cycle, but raises also key challenges for the specification of the social objective to be pursued by governments. Those challenges comprise the limits of utilitarianism when longevity varies, the distinction between luck and responsibility, and the opposition between the ex ante utilitarian approach and the ex post egalitarian one.

3.2.1 Inequality Aversion

A first important issue concerns the sensitivity of the social objective to the prevailing inequalities. True, that problem is a general one, and not specific to longevity inequalities. However, it nonetheless deserves particular attention, since, as we shall now see, standard social objectives may lead to quite counter-intuitive redistributive corollaries in the presence of inequalities in the human lifespan.

To illustrate this, let us assume that longevity is purely deterministic, and that there are two types of agent in the population: type-1 agents (who represent a proportion φ of the population) are long-lived, and type-2 agents (who represent a proportion $1 - \varphi$ of the population) are short-lived. All agents have standard, time-additive lifetime welfare. Each agent earns a wage w_i in the first period, supposed to be equal for the two types of agent: $w_1 = w_2 = w$. For simplicity, we assume all along that the total population is a continuum with a measure equal to 1 and that the length of the second period is unitary ($l = 1$).

At the laissez-faire level, type-1 agents smooth their consumption over their life cycle, whereas type-2 agents consume their whole income in the first period: $c_1 = d_1 = w/2 < c_2 = w$. There are, in general, large welfare inequalities at the laissez-faire level, because of Gossen's First Law (i.e., concavity of temporal welfare). Indeed, under general conditions identified in Leroux and Ponthière (2009), the long-lived agent enjoys a higher lifetime welfare than the short-lived agent: $u(w) < 2u(w/2)$. Given the absence of risk, welfare inequalities are merely due to the Law of Decreasing Marginal Utility: long-lived agents have, ceteris paribus, a higher capacity to spread their resources on different periods, implying a higher lifetime welfare.

Let us now see how a social planner would allocate those resources. To discuss this, let us start from a simple resource allocation problem faced by a classical utilitarian social planner, whose goal, following Bentham (1789), is to maximize the sum of individual utilities. The Benthamite social planner's problem can be written as:

$$max_{c_1,d_1,c_2} \varphi \left[u(c_1) + u(d_1)\right] + (1 - \varphi)u(c_2)$$

$$s.t. \varphi\, (c_1 + d_1) + (1 - \varphi)c_2 \le 2w.$$

The solution is:

$$u'(c_1) = u'(c_2) = u'(d_1) = \lambda$$

where λ is the Lagrange multiplier associated with the resource constraint. These equalities imply: $c_1 = c_2 = d_1 = \frac{2w}{3}$. Classical utilitarianism implies an equalization of consumptions for all life periods and all individuals. Hence, long-lived individuals, who benefit from an amount of resources equal to $\frac{4w}{3}$, receive twice more resources than the short-lived, who only receive $\frac{2w}{3}$. Classical utilitarianism thus implies a redistribution from the short-lived towards the long-lived. Note that, at the classical utilitarian optimum, the lifetime welfare inequalities between the long-lived and the short-lived are now larger than at the laissez-faire level: instead of an inequality:

$$2u(w/2) - u(w)$$

we now have, at the utilitarian optimum:

$$2u\,(2w/3) - u\,(2w/3)\,,$$

which is unambiguously larger. Hence classical utilitarianism implies here a double penalty for the short-lived: not only are the short-lived penalized by nature (as they enjoy, for an equal amount of resources, a lower lifetime welfare than the long-lived at the laissez-faire level), but they also suffer from a redistribution towards the long-lived. That redistribution from the short-lived towards the long-lived is counterintuitive. The only way to justify it is to say that type-1 agents at old age are different people from type-1 agents at a young age. But that kind of justification is far from straightforward. Another way to try to escape from that paradoxical redistribution is to opt for an alternative modeling of individual preferences, based on Bommier (2006, 2011a,b). If agents' lifetime welfare now takes the form of a concave transform $V(.)$ of the sum of temporal utilities, the laissez-faire level remains the same as above (as here longevity is purely deterministic), but the Benthamite social optimum is now obtained by solving the following problem:

$$max_{c_1,d_1,c_2} \varphi V\left[u(c_1) + u(d_1)\right] + (1 - \varphi)V\left[u(c_2)\right]$$

$$s.t. \varphi\, (c_1 + d_1) + (1 - \varphi)c_2 \le 2w.$$

This leads to the FOCs:

$$V'\left[u(c_1) + u(d_1)\right]u'(c_1) = \lambda\,,$$

$$V'\left[u(c_1) + u(d_1)\right]u'(d_1) = \lambda\,,$$

$$V'\left[u(c_2)\right]u'(c_2) = \lambda\,,$$

where λ is the Lagrange multiplier associated with the resource constraint. Given the concavity of $V(.)$, we now have: $c_1 = d_1 < c_2$, that is, the short-lived now have a higher consumption per period than the long-lived. Hence, lifetime welfare inequalities are here reduced in comparison to classical utilitarianism. In some sense, concavifying lifetime welfare is formally close to shifting from classical towards more inequality-averse utilitarianism, as suggested, among others, by Atkinson and Stiglitz (1980, pp. 339–40).

Note, however, that the concavification of lifetime utilities through the transformed $V(.)$ only mitigates the tendency of utilitarianism to redistribute from the short-lived towards the long-lived, but does not, in general, suffice to reverse the direction of redistribution. An alternative solution is thus needed. One remedy, based on Broome's (2004) attempt to provide a value to the continuation of life, consists of monetizing the welfare advantage induced by a longer life, and to count it as a part of the consumption enjoyed by the long-lived. As shown by Leroux and Ponthière (2010), that solution is close to the Maximin solution, that is, a social welfare function à la Atkinson, but with an infinite inequality aversion. Another remedy is the possibility of giving more social weight to the short-lived individuals relative to the long-lived ones, in such a way that in the first-best solution, there would be no transfer from the first to the second.

3.2.2 Responsibility and Luck

As shown earlier, longevity inequalities raise serious challenges to policy-makers even under standard consequentialist social objectives (such as utilitarian social objectives). But beyond individual outcomes in terms of longevity and consumption, one may argue that a reasonable social objective should also pay attention to how those outcomes are reached. In our context, this amounts to examining the reasons why some individuals turn out to be short-lived, while others turn out to be long-lived.

The underlying intuition, as advocated by Fleurbaey (2008), is the following. True, the idea of responsibility has remained surprisingly absent from important strands of normative thinking in political philosophy and welfare economics. However, as soon as we start living in a free society, where free individuals make decisions about, for instance, the goods they consume, the activities they take part in, the job for which they apply, etc., it seems hardly plausible to leave responsibility issues aside. Responsibility is a necessary consequence of any substantial amount of freedom. As such, whatever theorists think about responsibility or not, responsibility is part and parcel of any free society.

This is the reason why late twentieth-century egalitarian theories, such as the one advocated by Rawls (1971), are all, at least to some extent, relying on a distinction between what characteristics of situations are due to pure luck, and what characteristics are, on the contrary, due to individual choices, and, as such, involve their responsibility. That distinction between luck characteristics and responsibility characteristics is crucial for policy making. According to Fleurbaey (2008), welfare inequalities due to luck are characteristics ethically unacceptable, and, as such, invite a compensation: this is the underlying intuition behind the compensation principle ("same responsibility characteristics, same welfare"). However, welfare inequalities due to responsibility characterisitcs are ethically acceptable, and, thus, governments should not interfere with the latter type of inequalities: this is the natural reward principle ("same luck characteristics, no intervention").

The distinction between luck characteristics and responsibility characteristics is most relevant for the study of longevity inequalities. As shown by Christensen et al. (2006), the genetic background of individuals explains between one-quarter and one-third of longevity inequalities within any given cohort. Hence, given that individuals do not choose their own genetic background, a significant part of longevity inequalities lies outside their control. However, individuals can have also a significant influence on their survival chances, through their lifestyle. As shown by Kaplan et al. (1987) in their longitudinal study in California, individual longevity depends on eating behavior, drinking behavior, smoking, sleep patterns, and physical activity.

It follows from all this that longevity is partly a luck characteristic of the individual, and partly a responsibility characteristic. That double-origin of longevity inequalities leads us to a problem that is now well known in the compensation literature (see Fleurbaey & Maniquet 2004): it is impossible, under general conditions, to provide compensation for a luck characteristic without, at the same time, reducing inequalities due to responsibility characteristics. Hence, a choice is to be made between *compensation* and *natural reward*.

To illustrate this, consider the simple case where there are two groups of agents $i = 1, 2$, whose old age longevity l_i is a function of genes ε_i and health efforts e_i. Those agents differ in two aspects. On the one hand, agents of type-1 have better longevity genes than individuals of type-2. On the other hand, type-1 individuals have a lower disutility from effort than type-2 individuals. In that setting, the genetic background is a circumstance of luck characteristics, whereas the disutility of effort is a responsibility characteristics. For simplicity, longevity is assumed to be given by:

$$l_i = \varepsilon_i l(e_i)$$

with $l'(.) > 0$, and $l''(.) < 0$. We assume $\varepsilon_1 > \varepsilon_2$. The disutility of effort is:

$$v_i(e_i) = \delta_i v(e_i)$$

with $v'(.) > 0$, and $v''(.) > 0$. We assume: $\delta_1 < \delta_2$. At the laissez-faire level, agents solve the problem:

$$max_{c_i,d_i,e_i} u(c_i) - \delta_i v(e_i) + \varepsilon_i l(e_i) u(d_i)$$

$$s.t. c_i + \varepsilon_i l(e_i) d_i \leq w.$$

The FOCs yield, for agents of type-i = 1, 2:

$$c_i = d_i; \delta_i v'(e_i) = \varepsilon_i l'(e_i)[u(d_i) - u'(d_i)d_i].$$

Given $\varepsilon_1 > \varepsilon_2$ and $\delta_1 < \delta_2$, type-1 agents make, ceteris paribus, more effort than type-2 agents. If agents had the same genes ($\varepsilon_1 = \varepsilon_2$), it would still be the case that type-1 agents make more effort than type-2 agents. Alternatively, if they all had the same disutility of labour, type-1 agents would still make more effort (because of better genes).

Comparing their lifetime welfares, we expect that type-1 agents have, thanks to their better genes and lower disutility of effort, a higher welfare. Are those welfare inequalities acceptable? Yes, but only to a certain extent.

Note that, if all agents had the same disutility of effort (if $\delta_1 = \delta_2 = \bar{\delta}$), type-1 agents would still get a higher welfare, thanks to their better genes. Hence, the compensation principle ("same responsibility, same welfare") would require a redistribution from type-1 towards type-2, to obtain the equality:

$$u(c_1^*) - \bar{\delta}v(e_1^*) + \varepsilon_1 l(e_1^*)u(d_1^*) = u(c_2^*) - \bar{\delta}v(e_2^*) + \varepsilon_2 l(e_2^*)u(d_2^*).$$

As $\varepsilon_1 > \varepsilon_2$, we expect $c_1^* < c_2^*$ and/or $d_1^* < d_2^*$: some monetary compensation should thus be given to type-2 agents.

If all agents had equal genes (if $\varepsilon_1 = \varepsilon_2 = \bar{\varepsilon}$), type-1 agents would still, thanks to a lower disutility of effort, be better off than type-2 agents. But the principle of natural reward ("equal luck, no intervention") would regard those inequalities as acceptable, since these are not due to luck:

$$u(c_1^{**}) - \delta_1 v(e_1^{**}) + \bar{\varepsilon}l(e_1^{**})u(d_1^{**}) > u(c_2^{**}) - \delta_2 v(e_2^{**}) + \bar{\varepsilon}l(e_2^{**})u(d_2^{**}).$$

The problem is that the need to compensate for inequalities due to luck characteristics may clash with the noninterference on inequalities due to responsibility characteristics. To see this, suppose reference disutility $\bar{\delta} = \delta_1$ and reference genes $\bar{\varepsilon} = \varepsilon_1$. Then the above conditions become:

$$u(c_1^*) - \bar{\delta}v(e_1^*) + \bar{\varepsilon}l(e_1^*)u(d_1^*) = u(c_2^*) - \bar{\delta}v(e_2^*) + \varepsilon_2 l(e_2^*)u(d_2^*)$$
$$u(c_1^{**}) - \bar{\delta}v(e_1^{**}) + \bar{\varepsilon}l(e_1^{**})u(d_1^{**}) > u(c_2^{**}) - \delta_2 v(e_2^{**}) + \bar{\varepsilon}l(e_2^{**})u(d_2^{**}).$$

We see that those two conditions are, in some cases, incompatible. Indeed, the LHS of the two conditions are identical. Hence, if $\varepsilon_1 l(e_2^{**})u(d_2^{**}) - \varepsilon_2 l(e_2^*)u(d_2^*) > \delta_2 v(e_2^{**}) - \delta_1 v(e_2^*)$, we obtain a contradiction. Thus a given allocation may fail to satisfy both the compensation principle and the natu-ral reward principle. Such a conflict between compensation and reward is not uncommon when there is no separability between the contributions of effort and luck to individual payoffs. This is the case in our example, where type-1 agents, who have better genes than type-2 agents, also make greater efforts. Hence it is impossible to give them the reward for their efforts, and, at the same time, to compensate type-2 agents, since the latter compensation goes against rewarding effort.

3.2.3 Ex Ante versus Ex Post Equality

This treatment of longevity inequalities under utilitarianism is hardly defend-able, since individuals are here not responsible at all for inequalities in real-ized durations of life. Hence, if one follows Fleurbaey's theory of fairness (Fleurbaey 2008), those inequalities should be abolished by governments, since their victims can hardly be regarded as responsible for them. Therefore, it makes sense to consider an alternative social objective, which amounts to maxi-mizing the realized lifetime well-being of the short-lived persons. Fleurbaey et al. (2014) show that, once that social objective is adopted, it is possible for the social planner to abolish inequalities in realized lifetime well-being across short-lived and long-lived individuals, provided the available aggregate resources are sufficiently large so as to insure $u(c) > 0$ at all periods for all individuals. Under that social objective, the problem is:

$$max_{c,d} min \{\phi[u(c)], \phi[u(c) + lu(d)]\}$$

$$s.t. c + \pi ld = w.$$

The objective function is not differentiable, but this problem can be rewritten as the maximization of the well-being of the short-lived subject to the constraint that the long-lived is not worse-off than the short-lived:

$$max_{c,d} \phi[u(c)]$$

$$s.t. c + \pi ld = w$$

$$s.t. \phi[u(c) + lu(d)] \geq \phi[u(c)].$$

When the egalitarian constraint is binding, we have $u(d) = 0$, implying that old age consumption is fixed to the neutral level for continuing existence, i.e., to the level $\bar{c}$ such that $u(\bar{c}) = 0$. Then we have:

$$c = w - \pi l \bar{c}$$

$$d = \bar{c}.$$

Under that allocation, consumption profiles are strongly decreasing. This solution may look counterintuitive, but this is the price to pay to minimize inequalities in realized lifetime well-being across short-lived and long-lived individuals. Concentrating the consumption of resources early in life (when all individuals are still alive) allows to provide higher well-being levels at a young age for all individuals. More important, this will maximize the realized lifetime well-being of the unlucky short-lived.

Regarding the impact of the life horizon l, it follows from the above analysis that the larger l is, the less decreasing the optimal consumption profile will be. Thus, in comparison with the utilitarian social optimum, the parameter l here has an opposite effect on the slope of the socially optimal consumption profile.

If we turn back to the previous two-person example with risk neutrality with respect to the duration of life, the problem of the social planner is now:

$$max_{c_1,c_2,d_2} min\{u(c_1), u(c_2) + u(d_2)\}$$
$$s.t. c_1 + c_2 + d_2 = 2w.$$

The solution to that problem is:

$$c_1 = c_2 = (2w - \bar{c})/2$$
$$d_2 = \bar{c}.$$

Note that, at this allocation, there exists no inequality in lifetime well-being between the short-lived and the long-lived, since we have:

$$u\left(\frac{2w - \bar{c}}{2}\right) = u\left(\frac{2w - \bar{c}}{2}\right) + u(\bar{c})$$

since $u(\bar{c}) = 0$. Thus, contrary to what utilitarianism does, the ex post egalitarian optimum does not exacerbate well-being inequalities between short-lived and long-lived agents, but make these inequalities disappear.

This section shows that adopting a standard utilitarian social welfare function or, alternatively, the ex post egalitarian social welfare function, has significant consequences regarding the form of the social optimum. Note, however, that our discussion has concentrated mainly on a highly abstract resource allocation problem. The next section will explore policy issues that are closer to the ones faced by contemporary policy-makers.

4 Public Policy with Exogenous Longevity

Having examined some conceptual issues, we can now focus on the policy challenges raised by varying longevity. Actually, shifting from an economy with constant longevity to a more realistic economy with varying – and potentially unequal – longevity raises additional difficulties for the design of optimal public policy. As we will see, varying longevity tends to significantly complicate policy analysis in fields as diverse as labour market regulations, health policy, education policy, pensions, and the taxation of wealth and bequests. We start by looking at the impact of exogenous fertility on seven types of public policy.

4.1 Harsher Occupation and Shorter Life

Social security systems are under increased financing pressure due to the impact of population aging. With increasing life expectancy, it seems reasonable to require individuals to work longer. In recent years, several countries have increased the legal age of retirement and other countries are considering doing so. However, the chances of reaching and enjoying retirement in good health differ significantly across individuals. It has been shown that the chances of living longer and in good health are closely correlated with occupation. It would then seem natural to allow workers involved in harsh occupations to retire earlier than those who are engaged in safer occupations. This issue would be easy to cope with if there were a perfect correlation between occupation and longevity. In a two-occupation world, if all workers engaged in the harsher occupation were to have a higher mortality rate than the workers engaged in the safer occupation, one could easily design a social security scheme that would be more generous for the former. The problem gets more complicated in the realistic setting where the correlation is not perfect and when longevity is private information but occupation is observable. In such a setting, differentiating the pension policy by occupation would imply that the short-lived workers in the safe occupation would be mistreated.

We here follow Pestieau and Racionero (2016) who study the optimal design of pension schemes in an asymmetric information framework. We consider a society in which individuals differ in longevity and occupation. The longevity, represented by l_i, is private information. We assume that individuals can be either long-lived or short-lived: $\ell_L > \ell_S$, where L and S stand for long-lived and short-lived, respectively. The occupation, represented by subscript $j (j = 1, 2)$, is observable. n_j stands for the proportion of workers in occupation j and p_j represents the proportion of workers in occupation j who are short-lived. We assume that $p_1 > p_2$. Accordingly, we refer to occupation 1 as harsh and occupation 2 as safe. We take occupation as given and assume that both occupations yield the same wage w.[3] This assumption allows to focus on the effects of differential longevity on pension schemes and abstract from the standard redistribution associated with heterogeneous wages. Individuals live for two periods. In the first period, of length normalized to 1, individuals work full time and earn wage w, consume c_{ij}, and save s_{ij}. At some point in the first

---

[3] Note that although the age is the same in the two occupations, its expected value is lower in the harsher occupation.

period, individuals learn their longevity type. In the second period, of length l_i, individuals work for an endogenous amount of time z_{ij} and consume d_{ij}, which, in the absence of public pensions, is financed from their second-period earnings and savings (i.e., there are no bequests). Hence, there are four types of individual ij ($i = S, L; j = 1, 2$) with preferences represented by the following utility function:

$$U_{ij} = u(c_{ij}) + l_i u(d_{ij}) - v(z_{ij}; l_i)$$

where c_{ij} represents first-period consumption, d_{ij} represents second-period consumption, and z_{ij} represents second-period labour supply. The length of active life is therefore $1 + z_{ij}$. The utility function $u(.)$ of consumption in both first and second periods is assumed to be strictly increasing and concave. The disutility function of prolonged activity $v(z_{ij}; l_i)$ is assumed to be increasing and convex. We also assume that this disutility depends on the longevity of individuals l_i and, in particular, that the marginal disutility of working longer is higher for short-lived individuals: $v'(z; l_S) > v'(z; l_L)$ for all z.

We use the approach of optimal nonlinear taxation. This implies identifying the optimal bundle of consumption in both periods and retirement age for each type of individual, and showing how the optimal solution can be implemented via a nonlinear tax/transfer scheme. Accordingly, the social security policy consists of a bundle (c_{ij}, d_{ij}, z_{ij}) of consumption, in the first and second periods, and of labour supply in the second period (i.e., retirement age) for each individual ij. This social security policy can be implemented by a nonlinear tax on savings $t(s_{ij})$ and a nonlinear tax on prolonged activity $T(z_{ij})$. The consumer ij's problem under the nonlinear tax schedules $t(s_{ij})$ and $T(z_{ij})$ can be written as:

$$max_{s_{ij}, z_{ij}} u(w - s_{ij}) + l_i u(\frac{s_{ij} - t(s_{ij}) + wz_{ij} - T(z_{ij})}{l_i}) - v(z_{ij}; l_i).$$

If positive, the marginal tax, either $T'(z_{ij})$ or $t'(s_{ij})$ reflects a downward distortion in the choice of either the age of retirement or the amount of saving. A word is in order concerning the objective of the social planner. The traditional unweighted utilitarian social objective can have undesirable effects when longevity varies across individuals. Indeed, with additive utilities the utilitarian criterion implies redistribution from short- to long-lived individuals. Short-lived individuals are subject to a double penalty: they live fewer years and are made to subsidize those who live longer. In order to partially redress the implicit bias towards long-lived individuals that the unweighted utilitarian social objective entails, we incorporate social weights. We denote by γ_i the weight on individuals with longevity l_i ($i = S, L$). We assume $\gamma_S = \gamma \geq 1/2$

(and $\gamma_L = 1 - \gamma \leq 1/2$), where γ could be adjusted in such a way that the utilities of the two types are equalized if so desired. The Lagrangian for the second-best problem is:

$$\mathcal{L} = \sum_{j=1,2} n_j \{ \gamma_L (1-p_j)[u(c_{Lj}) + l_L u(d_{Lj}) - v(zj; \ell_L)]$$

$$+ \gamma_S p_j [u(c_{Sj}) + l_S u(d_{Sj}) - v(z_{Sj}; \ell_S)]\}$$

$$+ \mu \sum_{j=1,2} n_j \{(1-p_j)[(1+z_{Lj})w - c_{Lj} - l_L d_{Lj}]$$

$$+ p_j[(1+z_{Sj})w - c_{Sj} - l_S d_{Sj}]\}$$

$$+ \sum_{j=1,2} \lambda_j \{ u(c_{Lj}) + \ell_L u(d_{Li}) - v(z_{Li}; l_L) - u(c_{Si}) - l_L u(d_{Si}) + v(z_{Si}; l_L)\}$$

where the multipliers μ and λ_j are associated with the revenue and the self-selection constraint respectively. In setting the problem this way, we allow for different pension schemes in the two occupations. Otherwise, we would have a single self-selection constraint. By setting the $\lambda's$ equal to 0, we would get the first best outcome without any distortion.

From the FOCs, we obtain the following results. There is no distortion on long-lived workers in both occupations, but the particular bundle (c_{Lj}, d_{Lj}, z_{Lj}) and level of utility achieved by long-lived workers in occupation j depend on the proportions of short- and long-lived workers in each occupation. There are distortions at both margins – savings and prolonged activity – for short-lived workers in both occupations. The extent of the distortion, the particular bundle (c_{Sj}, d_{Sj}, z_{Sj}) and level of utility achieved depend on the proportions of short- and long-lived individuals in each occupation.

In this section, we deliberately did not consider the proposal of linking pension provisions to occupational status. This viewpoint is vindicated by Baurin (2021), who show that differences of life expectancy across socioeconomic status cannot be used for designing pension systems. This conclusion is due to the huge longevity variance within occupations observed in most countries, including the USA.

4.2 The Effect of Aging on the Distribution and Structure of Wealth

Following Piketty and his best-selling book *Capital in the Twenty-First Century* (2013), the role of inheritance in modern economies has increasingly come under scrutiny. Piketty observes a steady increase in the role of inherited wealth in total wealth as well as a deepening of wealth inequality. A natural question to be raised is whether demographic aging can explain those two evolutions.

Using a simple model, we show that both increasing longevity and decreasing fertility are likely to reduce the inherited share of total wealth. In other words, aging is not likely to explain the recent surge in this share in some advanced economies. We can also show that individual bequests will be more unequally distributed if aging is driven by a drop in fertility. In comparison, the effect of increasing longevity on the distribution of bequests is nonmonotonic.

Klimaviciute et al. (2019) use an OLG growth model with two periods. The first period has unitary length whereas the second period lasts $l < 1$; the probability to survive beyond the first period is π. We thus have two factors of longevity: an increase of either l or π. Given this survival uncertainty, we have two types of bequest: planned and unplanned. For the sake of simplicity, we assume away any annuitization of retirement saving. Aging is triggered by three factors: maximum length of life l, survival probability π, and fertility n. The objective is to study the steady state equilibrium values of capital, inherited wealth and wealth distribution and to analyze the impact of the different causes of aging on these values. To obtain analytical results, we have to resort to restrictive assumptions such as that of quasi linear utility, which implies just two types of agents per period.

We adopt the following utility for a member of generation t:

$$U_t = c_t + \pi l u(d_{t+1}) + \pi n v(b_{t+1}^l) + (1 - \pi) n v(b_{t+1}^E)$$

where

$$d_{t+1} = R_{t+1} s_t / l$$
$$b_{t+1}^l = R x_t / n$$
$$b_{t+1}^E = R(x_t + s_t)/n$$
$$c_t = w_t - s_t - x_t + B_t^j,$$

where c_t and d_{t+1} denote first- and second-period consumption. The wage rate is w_t and the interest factor R_t. Saving is denoted s_t and intended bequest x_t, whereas b_{t+1}^l is inheritance in case of long life of the parent and b_{t+1}^E, inheritance in case of early death of the parent. B_t^j stands for inherited wealth in case of early $(j = E)$ or late $(j = L)$ bequest. The utility functions are $u(.)$ with consumption as argument and $v(.)$ with bequests as arguments; they are both strictly concave.

Maximizing U_t with respect to s_t and x_t yields:

$$\frac{\delta U_t}{\delta s_t} = -1 + \left[\pi u'(d_{t+1}) + (1 - \pi) v'(b_{t+1}^E) \right] R_{t+1} = 0$$

$$\frac{\delta U_t}{\delta x_t} = -1 + \left[\pi v'(b_{t+1}^l) + (1 - \pi) v'(b_{t+1}^E) \right] R_{t+1} = 0.$$

Combining those two FOCs gives:

$$u'(d_{t+1}) = v'(b_{t+1}^{L})$$

which implies that x is a function of s:

$$x_t = \varphi_t = \varphi \left[s_t, R_{t+1}, \pi, l, n, I, a \right].$$

Capital accumulation is given by:

$$nk_{t+1} = s_t + x_t,$$

where n is the fertility rate but also $1+$ the rate of growth of population.

Assume now that $u = \ln; v = \beta \ln$. With this assumption, along with that of quasi linearity, the different sources of saving, x_t and s_t, are time invariant. The individual's problem is to maximize the following utility:

$$U_t = c_t + \pi \left[l \ln d_{t+1} + \beta n \ln b_{t+1}^{L} \right] + (1 - \pi) \beta n \ln b_{t+1}^{L}.$$

This gives the FOCs:

$$\frac{\delta U_t}{\delta s_t} = -1 + \frac{\pi l}{s_t} + \frac{(1 - \pi) n \beta}{x_t + s_t} = 0$$

$$\frac{\delta U_t}{\delta x_t} = -1 + \frac{\pi \beta n}{x_t} + \frac{\beta n (1 - \pi)}{s_t + x_t} = 0.$$

Then, we obtain:

$$\frac{n\beta}{x} = \frac{l}{s}$$

and

$$-s + \frac{(1 - \pi) n \beta}{1 + \frac{n\beta}{l}} + \pi l = 0.$$

Combining those two equations leads to:

$$s + x = \pi l + n\beta.$$

Then, capital accumulation is simple:

$$nk = \pi l + n\beta$$

and thus we have that k increases with β, π, l and decreases with n.

Let us denote the ratio of inherited wealth to total wealth by $\Theta = \frac{\pi s + x}{s + x}$. We thus get:

$$\Theta = \frac{\pi l + n\beta}{l + n\beta}.$$

This implies that the ratio Θ increases with the length of life and the survival probability but decreases with the fertility rate and the preference for bequests.

We now try to assess the impact of aging on the distribution of inherited wealth. Thanks to the quasi linear utility specification, there are two levels of inherited wealth in society: those of the children whose parent survived and those of the children whose parent did not survive. Inherited wealth is thus equal to $(s + x) R$ for a fraction $1 - \pi$ of heirs and xR for a fraction π. As indicator of inherited wealth inequality Φ, we use the coefficient of variation. We thus have:

$$\Phi = \frac{\sqrt{var(\omega)}}{\bar{\omega}},$$

where ω stand for inherited wealth: $\omega = \{(s + x) R, xR\}$. And thus:

$$\Phi = \frac{\sqrt{\pi (1 - \pi)}}{n\beta + (1 - \pi)}.$$

In other words, we observe that aging has a disequalizing effect for any value of n and for $\pi < 1/2$. The lifetime horizon has no effect on the Φ.

4.3 Longevity, Education, and Growth

Whereas there exist various engines of growth, a greater emphasis has, in recent decades, been laid on the crucial role played by education and human capital accumulation. Following the seminal contribution by Ben-Porath (1967), a great deal of attention was paid to the link between education, life expectancy, and growth. The canonical model used in this literature can be easily introduced.

Consider a small open economy where the wage rate and the gross interest rate are exogenously given. The gross rate of interest is equal to 1. An individual can live at most for two periods. In each "alive" period, he is endowed with one unit of time. In the first period, he works and earns $w(e)$ where $w(e)$ is strictly concave with e denoting the level of education. The income in the first period is used for consumption, c, saving s, and the (unitary) cost of education. Thus $c = w(e) - e - s$. Survival becomes uncertain at the end of the first period. Let $\pi \epsilon (0, 1)$ denote the probability of surviving into the second period. Contingent on survival, individuals divide the unit time endowment between leisure and working time, z. To facilitate interpretation, z can be considered as the age of retirement. Second-period consumption is denoted by $d = \frac{s}{\pi} + w(e)z$, where $1/\pi$ is the rate of return of the saving annuity. Denoting $v(z)$ the disutility of labor, the expected lifetime utility is represented by:

$$U = u(w(e) - e - s) + \pi \left[u \left(\frac{s}{\pi} + w(e)z \right) - v(z) \right].$$

Each individual maximizes U with respect to e, s and z. We obtain the following solutions for savings, retirement and schooling spending:

$$-u'(c) + u(s) = 0$$
$$u'(d)w(e) - v'(z) = 0$$
$$-u'(c)\left[w'(e) - 1\right] + \pi u'(d)w'(e)z = 0.$$

The last FOC can be rewritten as:

$$w'(e)\left(1 + \pi z\right) = 1.$$

This implies that an exogenous rise in the survival probability has a positive effect on schooling and a negative effect on the retirement age.

Assume now that the survival probability increases with the level of education, namely, $\pi = \pi(e)$ with $\pi'(e) > 0$. Then the above third FOC becomes:

$$\frac{\partial U}{\partial e} = u'(d)\left\{\left[w'(e)\left(1 + \pi(e)z\right) - 1\right] + \pi'(e)\left[\frac{u(d)}{u'(d)} - d\right]\right\} = 0.$$

One generally assumes as seen above that $\frac{u(d)}{u'(d)} - d > 0$. Assume further that this expression is constant and that $\pi(e) = \overline{\pi} + \alpha\phi(e)$ where $\alpha > 0$ measures the intensity of the effect of education on longevity. We can then show that: $\frac{de}{d\alpha} > 0$.

Using a three-period OLG model with education and fertility choices, Ehrlich and Lui (1991) showed that an improvement of survival conditions at a young age can, by reducing fertility, boost education and growth. Boucekkine et al. (2002) used a vintage human capital model to distinguish between three channels by which life expectancy affects human capital accumulation. First, a higher life expectancy raises the quantity of workers, by reducing the number of workers dying prematurely; second, a higher life expectancy induces more investment in education (i.e., the Ben-Porath effect). But in addition to these two positive effects, there is another, negative effect: the rise in life expectancy raises the average age of workers, which may reduce productivity and growth. More recently, various OLG models studied the existence of a feedback effect: not only does longevity affect education and growth, but also growth allows for more investment in health, leading to an improvement of survival conditions. Hence there exists some virtuous cycle, where better survival conditions lead to more education, and more education leads to better survival conditions. Models of that kind include, among others, Blackburn and Cipriani (2002) and Chakraborty (2004), where the child decides how much education to attend (de la Croix & Licandro 2013), where the education decision is taken by parents alone, and (Leker and Ponthière 2015), where education is the outcome of an intrafamily bargaining process between the parent and the child. But the interplay between longevity, education, and growth can also be studied from a policy perspective.

Besides the widely studied Ben-Porath conjecture, there are lots of studies both cross-sectional and intertemporal showing that education increases longevity. The latter effect can be explained by the fact that education implies better lifestyle, more emphasis on prevention, safer occupation. The crucial role played by education in this virtuous cycle suggests that inequalities in the capacity of children to convert educational effort into educational and professional achievements may be a key determinant of inequalities not only in income, but, also, in health and longevity. Nishimura et al. (2015) examine the design of the optimal public policy in an OLG economy where education affects life expectancy and where life expectancy affects education through the Ben-Porath effect. They consider a model in which young individuals borrow to fund their education, which will improve their future wage with some decay. They first reexamine the conditions under which an improvement in survival conditions raises education. Then, they consider the design of optimal public policy. Among the reasons for government intervention, there is the possibility that physical or human capital accumulation be suboptimal. Another reason is that, if agents are myopic, they can choose too little education and this calls for a Pigovian subsidy. There is also the objective of redistributing income across individuals having different learning capacities. With an utilitarian objective and asymmetric information, one ends up taxing the level of education of the individuals with the lower learning capacity. This implies, quite paradoxically, a widening of the longevity gap. Finally, note that those studies, which take place in dynamic OLG models, usually assume, for the sake of simplicity, risk neutrality with respect to the duration of life. The reason is that relaxing that assumption would make it difficult to derive a closed-form solution for the education investment, making the resolution of the dynamic system at least difficult, if not impossible. However, introducing some risk aversion with respect to the duration of life could, as stated earlier, affect the form of the relation between education and longevity.

4.4 Longevity, Pensions, and Growth

In addition to the link between education, longevity, and growth, great attention was also paid to the impact of longevity increase on capital accumulation and pensions. Demographic aging poses a major challenge to all industrialized economies and a large number of developing countries. Although an increase in the average age is a common trend around the world, the factors that lead to such changes vary across countries ; they can be traced back to decreases in fertility rates and increases in longevity, albeit at different magnitudes in different economies. There exist a number of studies investigating how institutional factors and behavioral responses may affect the impact of aging on capital accumulation. One interesting discussion on the effect of longevity increase on growth is provided by Bloom et al. (2007). These authors point out that, in theory, improvements in healthy life expectancy should generate increases in the average age of retirement, with little effect on savings rates. In many countries, however, retirement incentives in social security programs prevent retirement ages from keeping pace with changes in life expectancy, leading to an increased need for life-cycle savings. They empirically show that increased longevity raises aggregate savings rates in countries with universal pension coverage and retirement incentives. Similarly, Bloom et al. (2003) show that aging leads to more capital accumulation even if retirement is endogenous. Echevarria (2004) reaches the same conclusion.

Kalemli-Ozcan et al. (2000) show that the positive effect of mortality decline on capital accumulation is made larger if education decisions are endogenous. De la Croix and Licandro (1999) and Zhang et al. (2001, 2003) argue that the effect of increasing longevity depends on its initial level. For low levels of life expectancy the effect is positive but it can turn negative for high levels. Similarly, Miyazawa (2006) also shows that the effect of an increase in longevity on economic growth has a hump-shaped pattern. Increases in longevity can impact growth indirectly through the pay-as-you go social security system, whose return depends on both fertility and mortality. Among the studies that link the impact of aging with social security systems, Ito and Tabata (2008) find that the unfunded social security system provides a sufficient mechanism to have such a hump-shaped relationship between longevity and per capita output. Pestieau et al. (2008) study the design of the optimal preventive health spending in a second-best context where the replacement rate of the PAYG system is taken as given, and show that the optimal health subsidy is decreasing with the prevailing replacement rate. Tabata (2014) looks at the effect of a shift from a DB to a DC PAYG pension on growth. He shows that this shift is growth enhancing and alleviates the cost of aging. Heijdra and Mierau (2011) also compare the relative effects of DB and DC PAYG pensions on economic growth with aging. They show that the DC formula fares better that the DB one in facilitating growth. They also show that raising the retirement age as a response to an increase in longevity dampens the growth gains.

In the same vein, Dedry et al. (2015) provide a comparison of several different institutional settings, i.e., different social security systems and retirement age policies, and types of aging in a unified framework. Their main conclusion is that from the long-run welfare viewpoint, the ideal is a defined contribution scheme and a mandatory early retirement constraint. We now sketch their model. They use a standard two-period overlapping generation model. An individual who belongs to generation t lives in two periods: t and t + 1. The first period of their life has a unitary length, while the second one has a length l, where $l < 1$ reflects variable longevity. In the first period, the individual works and earns a wage, w_t, which is devoted to the first-period consumption, c_t, saving, s_t, and pension contribution, τ. In the second period, they work an amount of time $z_{t+1} < l$ and earns $z_{t+1}w_{t+1}$. These earnings, together with the proceeds of savings $R_{t+1}s_t$ and the PAYG pension p, finance the second-period consumption d_{t+1}. We assume that working in the second period z_{t+1} implies a disutility defined in monetary terms $v(z_{t+1}; l)$, where $v_z > 0$, $v_{zz} > 0$ are imposed for the existence of a unique solution. In addition, disutility from working in the second period of life is a decreasing function of longevity, i.e., $v_l < 0$, which reflects the idea that an increase in longevity fosters later retirement. Note that, for simplicity, earnings in the second period of life is not taxed. Intuitively, the end of the first period can be interpreted as the statutory age of retirement, unless otherwise indicated by an explicit mandatory retirement age. Any investment in funded social security system is not modeled explicitly, as it is assumed to be identical to other savings. Thus, the pension contribution parameter τ measures the relative size of the unfunded pensions. In other words, $\tau = 0$ implies that the whole pension system is funded. Denoting by $u(.)$ the utility function for consumption c or d, and U, the lifetime utility, the problem of an individual of generation t is:

$$max_{s,z}U_t = u(w_t - \tau_t, s_t) + \beta l u\left[\frac{w_{t+1}z_{t+1} + R_{t+1}s_t + p - v(z_{t+1}, l)}{l}\right]$$

where $p = \tau(1 + n)$ is the pension benefit in period $t + 1$ and β is the time discount factor. The gross rate of population growth $(1 + n)$ is equivalent to the number of children per individual in this setup. The argument of second-period utility is net amount of resources then available divided by the length of the second period. The first order conditions for lifetime utility maximization are simply given by:

$$v_z(z_{t+1}, l) = w_{t+1},$$
$$\beta R_{t+1}u'(d_{t+1}) - u'(c_t) = 0,$$

where c_t and d_{t+1} denote the first- and second-period consumption. The first condition shows that the marginal disutility from second-period work needs to be equal to the wage rate at the optimum. The second condition is the consumption Euler equation, and it shows that the individual cannot gain further utility by reallocating consumption between periods. In order to be able to show some of our results analytically, we will use simple functional forms for $u(.)$

Table 4 The effects of aging on equilibrium capital per worker

Aging	Standard case	Defined contribution	Defined benefit
		Mandatory retirement	
Decreasing fertility	>0	>0	$\gtreqless 0$
Increase in longevity	>0	$\gtreqless 0$	$\gtreqless 0$
		Optimal retirement age	
Decreasing fertility	>0	>0	$\gtreqless 0$
Increase in longevity	>0	$\gtreqless 0$	$\gtreqless 0$

and $v(.)$. Accordingly, we assume that the period utility function is logarithmic $u(x) = \ln x$, and the monetary disutility function is quadratic in its main argument $v(x) = x^2/2\gamma l$. One clearly sees from the latter functional form that the disutility of working longer can be mitigated by an increase in longevity. With this specification, one can obtain explicit form for the saving function as well as for the retirement age z. And using a Cobb Douglas production function, the problem can be solved explicitly for four regimes of social security depending on whether it rests on defined benefits or on defined contributions and whether the age of retirement can be chosen freely or is mandatory, fixed below the optimal level. Table 4 provides the effects of aging on capital accumulation in these four regimes.

The standard case without social security is that aging regardless of its source leads to more capital accumulation. With social security, we get the same positive effect in case of declining fertility and with DC. Increasing longevity is ambiguous but has a higher effect with mandatory retirement than with optimal retirement. With DB, both sources of aging have an ambiguous effect; but, again, the effect is higher with mandatory retirement than with optimal retirement. As we consistently assume dynamic efficiency, all things being equal, utility under optimal retirement is not necessarily higher than under mandatory retirement. This is mainly because mandatory early retirement induce higher saving and capital accumulation as desired consumption in the second period of a lifetime cannot be financed by extending work hours. As a result, mandatory early retirement presents a case that is closer to the golden rule than the optimal retirement. This is a standard second-best problem where a distortion makes a second distortion desirable.

4.5 Old Age Poverty Alleviation

The eradication of poverty continues to be a priority for policy-makers worldwide. At the same time, trends in population aging results in a strong need to understand and address poverty in the later life years. One should be careful when dealing with this issue. Because there is a positive correlation between income and longevity, the poverty one observes in the real world is quite different and generally lower than the rate of poverty one would experience if every individual were to benefit from the same longevity. In other words, income-differentiated mortality, by reducing the share of poor persons in the population, leads to what has been called the "mortality paradox": the worse the survival conditions of the poor are, the lower is the measured poverty. And this applies particularly to the older population.[4]

To illustrate the implication of this paradox for public policy, we take the simple case of an economy comprising two types of individuals: the poor, denoted 1 and the rich, denoted 2. There are N_1 poor and N_2 rich. They both may live two periods, the rich with certainty and the poor with the probability π_1 of surviving to the second period. The rich earn w_2 in the first period of their life. Besides consuming c_2 they save s_2 and pay a tax t. In the second period, they consume $d_2 = s_2$. The poor consume all their earnings w_1 in the first period and consume a basic pension p in the second one. Their survival probability depends on some public health spending h such that $\pi_1 = \pi(h)$ with $\pi'(h) > 0$. Finally, we have a revenue constraint $N_2 t = N_1 [h + \pi_1 p]$.

We assume that t is given and that p is always below the poverty rate. Thus the head count poverty rate at old age is given by: $H = \frac{\pi(h)N_1}{N_2 + \pi(h)N_1}$. It is quite clear that a government seeking to minimize either the poverty rate or the poverty gap should aim at $h = 0$. By the same token, assume instead that the government wants to maximize a utilitarian social welfare function. This amounts to choose the value of h that maximizes:

$$\pi(h)u(p) = \pi(h)u(\frac{g - h}{\pi(h)}),$$

where $g = \frac{N_2 t}{N_1}$. Assuming an interior solution, the optimal value of h is given by:

$$\pi'(h)\left[u(p) - u'(p)p\right] - u'(p) = 0.$$

The term in brackets is standard in the literature on optimal population. It is positive as long as $u(0) = 0$ and $u(p)$ is strictly concave. This term would push for the highest value of h. This will be avoided thanks to the last term that reflect the direct cost of health spending in terms of foregone consumption.

---

[4] See Lefèbvre et al. (2018, 2019a,b).

4.6 Social Insurance for Long-Term Care and for Old Age

Over the last few decades, all OECD member countries have experienced a huge increase in their life expectancy. With the growing fraction of the population reaching the age of eighty, we also observe that life expectancy in good health, namely without major incapacities, increases but at a much slower pace. We indeed know that more than one-third of those aged over eighty are dependent, namely experience difficulties in performing activities of daily living independently. Those two evolutions put pressure on governments to finance pensions and long-term care. For example, in Germany and in France, public pensions account for respectively 10.3 and 13.6 percent of GDP whereas public spending for LTC represent 1.3 percent of GDP in both countries. By all accounts, these figures do not seem to meet the needs of aging populations. Compared to pensions, long-term care seems to be neglected. The first reason for this state of affairs is that public pensions were introduced a long time ago, just after the Second World War, whereas the need for LTC appeared much later with the rapid increase of the very senior dependency ratio, namely the fraction of the population aged over eighty. The second reason is that, traditionally, long-term care is provided informally by the family. Even though this rate of informal caring is declining, it is tempting for budget constrained governments not to face up to their responsibilities. Quite clearly, the scarcity of public funds gives the impression that there is a trade-off in the financing of public pensions and social LTC insurance.

Following Nishimura and Pestieau (2021), we analyze such a trade-off from a normative viewpoint. The question raised is simple: in an arbitrage between the two schemes, which one should be given priority? We start with some stylized facts: survival probabilities increase with income whereas both conditional and unconditional probability of old age dependency decrease with income (see Lefèbvre et al., 2018). In a seminal paper, Rochet (1991) proves that a social insurance may be justified even when the insurance market is efficient and that, if there is a negative correlation between probability of loss and labor productivity, social insurance should provide a complete coverage for every household. The rationale behind Rochet's result is that redistribution through social insurance does not carry any distortion, which is not the case of income taxation. Rochet's model implicitly assumes away liquidity constraints. We here deal with two risks, one positively correlated to income, namely that of a too long life, and the other negatively correlated to income, that is old age dependency. Without liquidity constraint, we show that dependency should be fully covered and pensions not at all. Introducing liquidity constraints make things more complicated. To make our point, we use a simple model of a two-period economy with three states of nature: in the first period, people work and save; in the second period, if they survive, people retire in good health or they may enter a state of dependency. Society comprises a number of individuals who differ in their productivity and their probabilities of survival and dependency.

4.6.1 Individual Problem

The problem of each individual i is to maximize the following lifetime utility with respect to his saving s_i, his labor supply l_i and his purchase of long-term care insurance I_i. Namely:

$$Max_{s,l,I}U = u(w_il_i(1 - \tau) + a - s_i - I_i - v(l_i)) + \pi_ip_iH\left(\frac{s_i}{\pi_i}\right.$$

$$\left. + \frac{I_i}{p_i\pi_i} + g + b\right) + (1 - p_i)\,\pi_iu\left(\frac{s_i}{\pi_i} + b\right)$$

where $u(.)$ is the consumption utility function, $H(.)$, the LTC utility and $v(.)$, the disutility of labor expressed in monetary terms, w_i, is the wage rate, π_i, the survival probability, p_i, the dependency probability, τ, the payroll tax, g and b, respectively the public LTC benefit and the public pension, and finally a is a demogrant.

The FOCs are:

$$\frac{\partial U}{\partial s_i} = -u'(c_i) + p_iH'(m_i) + (1 - p_i)u'(d_i) \leq 0$$

$$\frac{\partial U}{\partial I_i} = -u'(c_i) + H'(m_i) \leq 0$$

$$\frac{\partial U}{\partial l_i} = u'(c_i)\left[w_i(1 - \tau) - v'(l_i)\right] = 0,$$

where c_i and d_i denote first- and second-period consumption and m_i, LTC spending.

The interior solutions for this problem are:

$$u'(c_i) = u'(d_i) = H'(m_i); v'(l_i) = w_i(1 - \tau). \tag{4}$$

However, with the introduction of social benefits b and g, it is possible and even likely that the low income agents are liquidity constrained.

4.6.2 Optimum With no Liquidity Constraints

We now express the problem of the government with the following Lagrangian $\mathcal{L}$, where we use the operator E for $Ex = \sum n_ix_i$ (n_i being the number of individuals of type i):

$$\mathcal{L} = E\{u(wl(1-\tau) + a - s - I - v(l)) + \pi p H(\frac{s}{\pi} + \frac{I}{p\pi} + g + b)$$

$$+ (1-p)\pi u\left(\frac{s}{\pi} + b\right)$$

$$- \mu\left[a + \pi b + \pi p g - \tau w l\right]\}.$$

The FOCs are:

$$\frac{\partial \mathcal{L}}{\partial a} = E\left[u'(c) - \mu\right] = 0$$

$$\frac{\partial \mathcal{L}}{\partial g} = E\left[\pi p H'(m) - \mu \pi p\right]$$

$$\frac{\partial \mathcal{L}}{\partial b} = E\left[\pi p H'(m) + \pi(1-p)u'(d) - \mu\pi\right]$$

$$\frac{\partial \mathcal{L}}{\partial \tau} = E\left[-u'(c)wl + \mu\left(wl + \tau w\frac{\partial l}{\partial \tau}\right)\right].$$

In compensated terms (compensation with a):

$$\frac{\partial \mathcal{L}^C}{\partial \tau} = \frac{\partial \mathcal{L}}{\partial \tau} + \frac{\partial \mathcal{L}}{\partial a}Ewl$$

$$= -cov(wl, u'(c)) + \mu\left(Ewl + \tau Ew\frac{\partial l}{\partial \tau}\right) = 0$$

$$\frac{\partial \mathcal{L}^C}{\partial g} = \frac{\partial \mathcal{L}}{\partial g} - \frac{\partial \mathcal{L}}{\partial a}E\pi p = E\pi p u'(c)) - E\pi p Eu'(c)$$

$$= cov(\pi p, u'(c)) > 0 \Longleftrightarrow Corr(\pi p, w) < 0$$

$$\frac{\partial \mathcal{L}^C}{\partial b} = \frac{\partial \mathcal{L}}{\partial b} - \frac{\partial \mathcal{L}}{\partial a}E\pi = E\pi u'(c) - E\pi Eu'(c))$$

$$= cov(\pi, u'(c)) < 0 \Longleftrightarrow Corr(\pi, w) > 0$$

where we use the equalities (4).

We thus have the result of Rochet: social insurance should be nil, if the correlation between the risk and the level of wage is positive; it can be as high as possible if this correlation is negative.

Consider now an increase of g compensated by a balanced budget decrease in b. This yields:

$$\frac{\partial \mathcal{L}^{CC}}{\partial g} = \frac{\partial \mathcal{L}}{\partial g} - \frac{\partial \mathcal{L}}{\partial b}\frac{E\pi p}{E\pi} = E\left[\pi p H'(m) - \frac{\pi p H'(m) + \pi(1-p)u'(d)}{E\pi}Ep\pi\right]$$

$$= \frac{1}{E\pi}\left[cov(u'(d), \pi p)E\pi - E\pi p cov\left(u'(d), \pi\right)\right] > 0. \tag{5}$$

It thus appears that, when there is no liquidity constraint, one should have a 100 percent public coverage of LTC and no public pensions. It is always socially desirable to increase LTC benefits at the expense of public pensions.

4.6.3 Optimum With Liquidity Constraints

We now introduce the possibility of liquidity constraints. The FOCs can now be written as:

$$\frac{\partial \mathcal{L}^C}{\partial g} = E\pi p H'(m) - E\pi p E u'(c)$$

$$= cov(\pi p, H'(m)) + E\pi p E\left[H'(m) - u'(c)\right] \tag{6}$$

$$\frac{\partial \mathcal{L}^C}{\partial b} = E\left[\pi p H'(m) + \pi(1-p)u'(d) - u'(c)E\pi\right] = \tag{7}$$

$$= cov\left(\pi p, H'(m)\right) + cov\left(\pi(1-p), u'(d)\right)$$

$$+ E\pi p\left[E H'(m) - u'(d)\right] + E\pi E\left[u'(d) - u'(c)\right]$$

$$\frac{\partial \mathcal{L}^{CC}}{\partial g} = \frac{1}{E\pi}E\left[\pi p H'(m)E\pi - \pi p H'(m)E\pi p - \pi(1-p)u'(d)E\pi p\right] =$$

$$= \frac{E\pi(1-p)}{E\pi}\left[cov(\pi p, H'(m)) - \frac{E\pi p}{E\pi(1-p)}cov(\pi(1-p), u'(d))\right.$$

$$\left. + E\pi p E\left[H'(m) - u'(d)\right]\right] \tag{8}$$

where the superscript C means that the public benefit is compensated by the demogrant whereas the superscript CC means that the increase in the benefit g is compensated by a decrease in the benefit b.

Let us first interpret (8) and compare it with (5). The covariance terms are the same and indicate that it is desirable to increase g at the expense of b. The last term of (8) makes all the difference. It reflects the existence of liquidity constraints. To better interpret it, we take explicit forms for the utility functions: $u(x) = Ax - 0.5x^2$; $H(x) = A(x-L) - 0.5(x-L)^2$, where L can be viewed as the basic LTC expenses. With these functions, we have for each i:

$$\Delta_i = H'(m_i) - u'(d_i) = -m_i + L + d_i = L - g - \frac{l_i}{\pi_i}$$

in the case of liquidity constraint for l_i, $\Delta_i = L - g_i$. From (8), it is clear that it is socially desirable to substitute public pensions for public LTC as long $g_i - L$ is not big enough to compensate for the first two terms that are positive.

L reflects the cost of LTC beyond standard consumption. If L were small, it would always be desirable to choose public LTC over public pensions. The optimal levels of g and b are given by equations (6) and (7). The equity term in (6) is unambiguously positive, which means that the level of g should increase as long as the liquidity constraint term is not to high. In (7), the equity term is ambiguous with one positive variance and a negative one. This means that the optimal level of b is likely to be much smaller relative to g. Indeed, it can be attained even with positive saving by everyone.

We can thus conclude that when there are liquidity constraints, it is socially desirable to substitute public pensions for long-term care as long as the liquidity constraints term does not dominate the two equity terms. The optimal level of public pensions can be attained with positive saving whereas the optimal amount of public LTC requires that at least some individuals do not buy LTC insurance.

4.7 Inheritance Taxation Related to Age and Dependency

The stylized facts used in the previous section can also be used to see whether the inheritance tax rates should vary with the age of the deceased. Wealth transfer taxation taxation has never been as unpopular as it is today. Half of OECD members countries have abolished it. Among them, one finds social democratic Sweden and Norway, Canada, and Austria. In OECD countries, the proportion of total government revenues raised by such taxes has fallen since the 1960s from over 1 percent to less than 0.5 percent.[5] There is a real puzzle over why inheritance taxes are unpopular relative to other taxes, since they are progressive and, assuming they are spent wisely on welfare goods, more people should gain than lose through inheritance tax. One of the main reasons why inheritance tax might be unpopular is its design.[6] This section addresses one issue concerning the design of the inheritance tax, namely whether the tax rates should vary with the age of the deceased. This question has been dealt with by Vickrey (1945), who was concerned by the fact that the tax burden was decreasing with the spacing between the occurrences of inheritance. He thus proposed to relate the tax to the number of years during which donors hold their wealth. In this section that follows Leroux and Pestieau (2021), we study whether inheritance taxation should vary depending on the age of the deceased and on the state of their health. We distinguish three types of bequest, depending or whether they are early, late in good health, or late in disability. We tackle this problem using the nonlinear tax approach. Following Atkinson and Stiglitz (1980), we know that if we have an optimal income taxation, there is no need for any additional tax. At the same time, we here have a setting where individuals differ not only in their productivity but also in their risk of early mortality or of a long life of disability. A tax or a subsidy on bequests can be desirable depending on the relation between these risks and earning. On this, we rely on the stylized facts of the previous section that the correlation between income and survival probability is positive, whereas the correlation between income and dependency probability is negative.

---

[5] OECD (2018).
[6] For a survey of the literature, see Cremer and Pestieau (2006).

Our society comprises N types of individual. They all live at most two periods, the first period with certainty but the second is uncertain. Further, this second period can be healthy or not. Each type is characterized by a wage w_i, a survival probability π_i, and a dependence risk p_i. Each individual supplies an amount of labor, l_i, which implies a disutility $h(l_i)$. Out of wage earnings, $y_i = w_i l_i$ each individual finances present consumption c_i, planned bequest b_i, and saving s_i for future consumption and possibly long-term care. Consumption utility is denoted $u(c_i)$ and $u(d_i)$, where d_i represents future consumption. Inheritance utility is denoted $v(b_i^j)$ where $j = E, L, D$ stand for the type of bequests (early, late in good health, dependent). It is increasing and concave in its arguments. Finally, $H(m_i)$ denotes the utility of elderly individuals when dependent and has, for argument's sake, longterm care spending m_i. $H(.)$ is also concave and such that $H(z) < u(z)$. Throughout the section, we assume that the rate of interest is zero. Assuming away any market for annuities and long-term care (LTC), the problem of each individual i amounts to maximizing the following expression:

$$U_i = u(w_i(l_i - s_i - b_i) - h(l_i) + \pi_i p_i [H(s_i) + v(b_i)] + (1 - \pi_i)v(b_i + s_i)$$
$$+ \pi_i(1 - p_i) [u(s_i - x_i) + v(x_i + b_i)]$$

where x_i is the fraction of saving that the healthy individual bequeath to their heir.

This lifetime utility can also be written as:

$$U_i = u(c_i) + \pi_i p_i [H(m_i) + v((b_i^D))] + \pi_i(1 - p_i) [u(d_i) + v((b_i^L))]$$
$$+ (1 - \pi_i)v(b_i^E)$$

where $b_i^E = (b_i + s_i); b_i^L = (b_i + x_i); b_i^D = b_i$ denote the three different types of bequest.

Two words of clarification on this specification are in order. First, we purposely assume that there is no LTC insurance or annuity market. As a consequence, in case of early death, parents leave an amount s of unplanned bequests besides the planned bequest b and individuals choose a saving level higher than what would be needed if $p = 0$, thus leaving an additional transfer x to their children in the case that they are healthy. We are thus left with different levels of bequests in the three states of the world and any optimal policy will try to reduce the gap between those bequests. Second, we deliberately opted for a particular type of intended bequests, namely that which arises from the joy of giving motivation.[7]

---

[7] See Piketty and Saez (2013).

We assume that the only variables that can be observed are the three different types of bequest, gross earnings $y_i = w_i l_i$, and consumption c_i.

We can express the individual lifetime utility in terms of these variables:

$$U_i = u\left[y_i - \theta(y_i) - b_i^E - \theta(b_i^E)\right] - h\left(\frac{y_i}{w_i}\right)$$
$$+ \pi_i p_i \left[H(b_i^D - b_i^D - \theta(b_i^D)) + v(b_i^D)\right]$$
$$+ \pi_i(1 - p_i)\left[u(b_i^E - b_i^L - \theta(b_i^L)) + v(b_i^L)\right] + (1 - \pi_i)v(b_i^E)$$

where we have introduced nonlinear taxes $\theta(.)$.

From the FOCs, we obtain the relevant marginal rates of substitution and the marginal tax rates, if any:

$$u'(c_i)[1 - \theta'(y_i)] = \frac{1}{w_i}h'\left(\frac{y_i}{w_i}\right); 1 + \theta'(b_i^E)$$
$$= \frac{\pi_i p_i H'(m_i) + \pi_i(1 - p_i)u'(d_i)) + (1 - \pi_i)v'(b_i^E)}{u'(c_i)}$$
$$1 + \theta'(b_i^L) = \frac{v'(b_i^L)}{u'(d_i)}; 1 + \theta'(b_i^D) = \frac{v'(b_i^D)}{H'(m_i)}.$$

To keep the presentation simple, we restrict the analysis to two types with $w_2 > w_1$. Thus individual 2 has a higher survival probability and a lower dependence probability than individual 1. This implies that the first-best solution is not sustainable as individual 2 will be tempted to mimic individual 1. We can now express the optimality problem of an utilitarian government as the maximization of the following Lagrangian expression in terms of the observable variables, namely, the three different types of bequest, gross earnings $y_i = w_i l_i$, and consumption c_i:

$$\mathcal{L} = \sum_{1,2}[u(c_i)) - h\left(\frac{y_i}{w_i}\right) + \pi_i p_i \left[H(b_i^E - b_i^D) + v(b_i^D)\right]$$
$$+ \pi_i(1 - p_i)\left[u(b_i^E - b_i^L) + v(b_i^L)\right] + (1 - \pi_i)v(b_i^E) - \mu\left(c_i + b_i^E - y_i\right)]$$
$$+ \lambda\left[u(z_2 - h\left(\frac{y_2}{w_2}\right)) + \pi_2 p_2 \left[H(b_2^E - b_2^D) + v(b_2^D)\right]\right.$$
$$\left. + \pi_2(1 - p_2)\left[u(b_2^E - b_2^L) + v(b_2^L)\right] + (1 - \pi_2)v(b_2^E)\right]$$
$$- \lambda\left[u(z_1 - h\left(\frac{y_1}{w_2}\right)) + \pi_2 p_2\left[H(b_1^E - b_1^D) + v(b_1^D)\right]\right.$$
$$\left. + \pi_2(1 - p_2)[u(b_1^E - b_1^L) + v(b_1^L)] + (1 - \pi_2)v(b_1^E)\right].$$

In this expression, μ is the multiplier associated with the resource constraint that amounts to the equality between aggregate earnings and both consumption and early bequest $(b + s)$ and λ is the multiplier associated with the self-selection constraint.

The FOCs of this problem with $\lambda = 0$ (perfect information) yield the first-best conditions:

$$u'(c_i) = \mu \tag{9}$$

$$h'(l_i) = \mu w_i \tag{10}$$

$$\pi_i p_i H'(b_i^E - b_i^D) + \pi_i(1 - p_i)u'(b_i^E - b_i^I) + (1 - \pi_i)v(b_i^E) = \mu \tag{11}$$

$$H'(b_i^E - b_i^D) + v'(b_i^D) = 0 \tag{12}$$

$$u'(b_i^E - b_i^I) + v'(b_i^I) = 0. \tag{13}$$

Before interpreting these conditions, it is important to note that these first-best conditions are constrained by the absence of insurance mechanisms. This implies that instead of the equality $b_i^E = b_i^I = b_i^D = b$, which would be obtained with these insurance devices, we have condition (11) that establishes an equality between the marginal utility of first-period consumption $u'(c_i) = \mu$ and the weighted average of the marginal utilities of bequests. Comparing these conditions with those of the laissez-faire level, we see that the first-best condition can be decentralized with just the use of interpersonal lump-sum transfers.

With $\lambda > 0$, we obtain the second-best solutions. One may easily check that there will be no distortion for individual 2. In other words, the above first-best conditions (9)-(13) apply. As to individual 1, some of his choices will be distorted as we now see from the FOCs:

$$u'(c_1)(1 - \lambda) - \mu = 0 \tag{14}$$

$$-h'(\frac{y_1}{w_1})\frac{1}{w_1} + \mu + \lambda h'(\frac{y_1}{w_2})\frac{1}{w_2} = 0; \tag{15}$$

$$\pi_1 p_1 H'(b_1^E - b_1^D) + \pi_1(1 - p_1)u'(b_1^E - b_1^I) + (1 - \pi_1)v(b_1^E) - \mu$$
$$-\lambda\left[\pi p_2 H'(b_1^E - b_1^D) + \pi_2(1 - p_2)u(b_1^E - b_1^I) + (1 - \pi_2)v(b_1^E)\right] = 0 \tag{16}$$

$$\pi_1 p_1\left[H'(b_1^E - b_1^D) + v'(b_1^D)\right] - \lambda\pi_2 p_2\left[H'(b_1^E - b_1^D) + v'(b_1^D)\right] = 0 \tag{17}$$

$$\pi_1(1 - p_1)\left[u'(b_1^E - b_1^I) + v'(b_1^I)\right] - \lambda\pi_2(1 - p_2)\left[u'(b_1^E - b_1^I) + v'(b_1^I)\right]$$
$$= 0 \tag{18}$$

Using the following notation $A = \pi_1 p_1 H'(b_1^E - b_1^D) + \pi_1(1 - p_1)u'(b_1^E - b_1^I) + (1 - \pi_1)v(b_1^E)$ and $B = \left[\pi p_2 H'(b_1^E - b_1^D) + \pi_2(1 - p_2)u(b_1^E - b_1^I) + (1 - \pi_2)v(b_1^E)\right]$, we can rewrite (23) as:

$$A = u'(c_1)(1 - \lambda) + \lambda B. \tag{19}$$

Equation (14)-(15) can be combined to obtain the standard taxation of wage earnings as in Atkinson and Stiglitz (1980) with $\theta'(y_1) > 1$. The two equations

(17) and (18) imply that there are no distortions in the choice of b_1^D and b_1^L. In other words, $\theta'(b_1^L) = 0$ and $\theta'(b_1^D) = 0$. As to the choice of b_1^E, rearranging equation (26), one gets:

$$1 + \theta'(b_1^E) = \frac{A}{u'(c_1)} = 1 - \lambda + \lambda \frac{B}{u'(c_1)} \tag{20}$$

where $1 + \theta'(b_1^E)$ is the marginal rate of substitution between c_1 and b_1^E that reveals the presence and the direction of the distortion.

Not surprisingly, when $\lambda = 0$, $\theta'(b_1^E) = 0$. Also when the probabilities of survival and of dependency are the same for the two types of individual, $A = B$ and $\theta'(b_1^E) = 0$. We now consider the case when A and B are different. Let us denote the difference between those two terms, by D, namely $D = B - A$. From (27), we write:

$$\theta'(b_1^E) = \frac{D\lambda}{A - B\lambda}$$

where the denominator of the RHS is equal to μ and is thus positive. The sign of the tax thus depends on the sign of D that can be expressed as:

$$D = (\pi_2 p_2 - \pi_1 p_1) \left[v'(b_1^D) - v'(b_1^L) \right] + (\pi_1 - \pi_2) \left[v'(b_1^E) - v'(b_1^L)) \right].$$

All the components of this equality can be signed : $\pi_2 p_2 - \pi_1 p_1 < 0, v'(b_1^D) - v'(b_1^L) > 0, \pi_1 - s\pi_2 < 0, v'(b_1^E) - v'(b_1^L) < 0$.

One expects D to be positive, which would imply that early bequests should be taxed. We can thus obtain the following conclusion. When the probabilities are identical across individuals, we have the Atkinson-Stiglitz result that when productivity is the only unobservable characteristic, an optimal income tax suffices to attain social optimality. When the probabilities differ, their proposition does not hold any more. Taxing early bequests contributes to the relaxation of the self-selection constraint.

5 Public Policy With Endogenous Longevity

In the previous section, we analyzed the public policy implications of exogenous longevity. We now turn to another set of issues that arise when fertility changes are the responsibility of either individuals or governments. We now look at the impact of endogenous fertility on seven types of public policy.

5.1 Optimal Taxation With Heterogeneity in Longevity Genes and Labor Productivity

One ongoing question in public finance is whether capital income should be taxed or not. In a full information world, there is no need to tax capital. Income taxation suffices. However, when the productivity of individuals is not observable and longevity is correlated with productivity, then it might be desirable to tax capital income. The high productive individuals living longer and thus saving more, capital income gives a signal of productivity. To show this point, we consider a two-period model, where agents live a first period (of length normalized to 1) with certainty, but enjoy a second period of life, also of unitary length, with a probability π. Agents are characterized by their productivity w and their survival probability that is positively correlated with w. The problem of individual i is to maximize the following lifetime utility:

$$U_i = u(c_i) - v(z_i) + \pi_i u(d_i),$$

where $v(z_i)$ denotes the disutility of working in the first period. Labor supply is given by z_i. Assume for the sake of simplicity that we have just two individuals 1 and 2 such that $w_2 > w_1$ and $\pi_2 > \pi_1$. We consider two cases. In the first, the government observes the two types and acts accordingly. In the second, it has to choose an allocation such that type-2 individual is not tempted to mimic type-1. This implies the following self-selection constraint:

$$u(c_2) - v(y_2/w_2) + \pi_2(d_2) \geq u(c_1) - v(y_1/w_2) + \pi_2(d_1)$$

where $y_i = z_i w_i$ denotes gross earning income. Assuming an utilitarian objective, the problem for the government is to find the values of y, c and d that maximize the following Lagrangian expression:

$$\mathcal{L} = \sum_{1,2} [u(c_i) - v(y_i/w_i) + \pi_i(d_i) - \mu\,(c_i + \pi_i d_i - y_i)]$$
$$+ \lambda\,[u(c_2) - v(y_2/w_2) + \pi_2 u(d_2) - u(c_1) + v(y_1/w_2) - \pi_2 u(d_1)]$$

where the Lagrange multipliers μ and λ are respectively associated with the resource constraint and the self-selection constraint. In the case of perfect observability, namely $\lambda = 0$, we obtain from the FOCs:

$$u'(c_i) = u'(d_i) = -v'(z_i)/w_i = \mu.$$

Consumptions are equalized between the two types and type-2 supplies more labor than type-1. There is no distortion in the choice of consumption and of labor supply. This optimum can be decentralized by simply transferring resources from type-2 to type-1. When the types cannot be observed, we still do not have distortion regarding type-2. However, type-1 is going to face a tax on both labor and capital income. These taxes contribute to satisfy the above self-selection constraint. These taxes imply the following distortion on the choice of saving and of labor:

$$\frac{u'(c_1)}{u'(d_1)} < 1; \frac{v'(z_1)}{u'(c_1)} < w_1.$$

The first inequality implies that capital income should be taxed.[8] The second is the standard taxation of earnings.

In this presentation, longevity is given. Leroux et al. (2011a,b) study this problem of optimal taxation with endogenous longevity. They analyze the optimal nonlinear tax-transfer policy in an economy where the two agents differ in productivity and in genetic background, and where longevity depends on health spending and genes. Assuming that e stands for health spending and ε for the longevity genes, the survival probability can be expressed as:

$$\pi_i = \pi(e_i, \varepsilon_i).$$

And the lifetime utility of an individual i can be written as:

$$U_i = u(c_i) - v(z_i) + \pi(e_i, \varepsilon_i)u(d_i).$$

The resource constraint is now:

$$\sum_{1,2}[c_i + e_i + \pi(e_i, \varepsilon_i)d_i - w_i z_i] = 0.$$

Leroux et al. (2011a) analyze the second-best optimality conditions when the government does not observe the two characteristic w_i and ε_i, but observes e_i, s_i, y_i. In this setting, one has to find the optimal tax on labor and capital income and also on health spending. Not surprisingly, the level and the size of these taxes depend on the distribution of the two characteristics, w_i and ε_i, as well as on the substitutability between e_i and ε_i in the survival function. They make the assumptions that e_i and ε_i are complements and that the type-2 agent would mimic the type-1 agent. Two cases can be considered. First, there is a negative correlation between genetics and productivity. Second, there is a positive correlation between genetics and productivity, but the productivity gap dominates the genetic gap. In both cases, the type-2 individual is not taxed. Under the first case, the type-1 individual is subject to a tax on labor income but to a subsidy on health spending and saving. Under the second case, this individual is subject to a tax on the three variables. This last result is surprising. One generally expects a subsidy on health spending. Under the second case, the tax on health expenditure is used to induce type-2 individual to reveal his true type and deter him from mimicking type-1 individual. Note that there are many reasons for subsidizing health expenditure that could lead to reverse this recommendation. For example, in case of misperception of the beneficial

---

[8] See Diamond and Spinnewijn (2011).

Table 5 Signs of taxes in the second-best
with $\pi_{\varepsilon e} > 0$

Taxes on	$\mathrm{Corr}(\varepsilon, w) > 0$	$\mathrm{Corr}(\varepsilon, w) < 0$
e_1	+	−
e_2	0	0
s_1	+	−
s_2	0	0
y_1	+	+
y_2	0	0

effect of preventive health expenditure, one could end up with a subsidy on health. Table 5 gives the sign of different taxes for the case of complementarity between ε and e. As expected, the type-2 individual is never taxed.

5.2 Preventive and Curative Health Care

As has already been alluded to, rationality or farsightedness can contribute to a longer life and a better health. The possibility to invest in one's future health raises some important challenges from a policy perspective. A well-known challenge consists of the choice of an optimal balance between preventive and curative health expenditures. Should the state spend more on prevention and less on curative expenditures, or the opposite? That question is a complex one, and the answer depends on the underlying assumption on individual rationality. The preventive versus curative dilemma was studied by Cremer et al. (2012) in an economy where individuals live for two periods. The first one is of length one and the second has a length that depends on private investment in health and on some "sinful" consumption in the first period (i.e., alcohol, cigarettes, junk food, etc.). Reducing sinful consumption, namely adopting an healthier life-style can be interpreted as having a preventive behavior. The lifetime welfare of individuals takes here the following form:

$$u(c) + \varphi(x) + l(\alpha x, e)u(d)$$

where x is the sin good, $\varphi(x)$ is the utility from sin good consumption at the young age, whereas e is the amount of curative health spending. We expect that the length of the second period increases with e and decreases with x: $l_{\alpha x} < 0, l_e > 0$. The parameter α denotes the degree of farsightedness (rationality). Some individuals may well perceive the impact of the consumption of sin good on their future health and longevity, in which case α is equal to one. But obviously not all agents are farsighted and many have an $\alpha < 1$. In this simple model, x is chosen in the first period and e at the beginning of the second period. The rate of interest is assumed to be zero. In the first period, the individual faces the budget constraints

$$c + x + s = w; d + e = s/l.$$

Maximizing their lifetime utility subject to these budget constraints, we obtain the following FOCs:

$$u'(c) = u'(d); \varphi'(x) = u'(c) - \alpha\varphi_{\alpha x}.$$

With $\alpha < 1$, we obtain a level of saving that is lower and a level of sin consumption that is higher than in the case $\alpha = 1$. At the start of the second period, the individual allocates the proceeds of his saving between consumption d and curative health spending, e, such that:

$$l_e(x, e)u(d) = l(x, e)u'(d).$$

Note that in the second period, when choosing d and e, the individual is assumed to use the correct longevity function $l(x, e)$. This is not necessarily the case. They could stick to their misperception, in which case the second-period FOC would be:

$$l_e(\alpha x, e)u(d) = l(\alpha x, e)u'(d).$$

In the real world, some people clearly perceive the impact of their lifestyle on their longevity. They anticipate correctly the effect of their healthy lifestyle in the first period on the length of the second. Other people do not anticipate correctly the impact of their sin consumption. Cremer et al. (2012) study the design of the optimal public intervention when agents differ in terms of their farsightedness. They show that sin goods should be taxed, to an extent that depends on individual myopia/ignorance. They also find that prevention should be encouraged, but that curative expenditures should not necessarily be encouraged. In particular, when individuals are myopic, it is not necessarily the case that curative health spending should be subsidized. Two cases can occur. In the first case, individuals acknowledge and regret their past mistake once they are in the second period of their life. In the second case, there is no regret. Cremer et al. show that, in the first case, curative health care does not need to be subsidized. However, individual savings should be subsidized in that case. The underlying intuition is that individuals who realize their mistakes in the second period will then optimally allocate their savings between either consumption or curative spending. By way of contrast, if we focus now on the second case, when individuals formulate no regret, and keep ignoring the impact of their behavior on their longevity, the government needs to subsidize curative spending, so as to decentralize the first-best optimum.

Once heterogeneity concerns both rationality and earnings, restoring the first-best optimum becomes even more difficult. Note that, among the two cases considered in Cremer et al. (2012), the prevalence of regret is the most widespread. Recent surveys showed that about 85 percent of smokers aged sixty-five and over regret having started to smoke, in the sense that, if they could change the past, they would not have started to smoke (see Slovic 2001; Jarvis et al. 2002; Fong et al. 2004). Hence, when calibrating the optimal sin tax formula, it should be kept in mind that the proportion of individuals formulating regrets strongly dominates the proportion of individuals ignoring mistakes. This pushes towards a larger taxation of sin goods ceteris paribus.

In the above presentation we have focused on sin goods. As already mentioned, reducing the consumption of sin goods can be interpreted as a preventive behavior towards a longer and healthier life. Taxation is one among other instruments that governments may use when agents make choices having long-term detrimental effects on their life expectancy. In some instances, particularly in case of emergency, direct compulsory measures have to be preferred. The COVID-19 pandemic is a good example. It provides a clear illustration of a trade-off between curative and preventive measures and of the way national governments addressed this trade-off. In a nutshell, the choice governments faced was between a costly policy of prevention and painful treatment for those infected by the virus. For countries that chose to adopt a preventive approach, the cost was huge in terms of GDP loss and the psychological burden of a lockdown. At the same time, they avoided thousands of death and unbearable suffering for those who had to be intubated. In all countries that resorted to strict lockdown, it is clear that the scales tilted in favor of prevention. We come back on this issue in Section 5.6.

5.3 Free-Riding and Longevity

Besides the prevention versus curation issue, the endogeneity of longevity also raises other challenges. The previous section considered individuals who may not be able to fully understand or internalize the impact of their behavior on their own future longevity, because of some myopia or ignorance. It should be stressed, however, that longevity-related choices affect not only individual well-being, but tend also, through various channels, to influence the well-being of society as a whole. Those other influences may, here again, not be fully taken into account by individuals when making longevity-affecting choices, perhaps because of conscious free riding. To illustrate this, it is relevant to make a parallel with fertility decisions. Fertility choices are made by parents, but those choices affect society as a whole, through lots of externalities, which can be either positive – through intergenerational transfers (Samuelson 1975) or scale effects (Kremer 1994) – or negative – through congestion or pollution. Adding some new living beings involves many effects, which are usually not taken into account by parents. The same problem arises regarding longevity-enhancing decisions. Indeed, although investing in one's health does not add a new person, it definitely adds some life years to the population, yielding positive or negative externalities. This fact was first highlighted by Davies and Kuhn (1992) and by Becker and Philipson (1998). As shown by those authors, individuals do not necessarily take into account, when making longevity-enhancing choices such as preventive spending, the negative impact of those decisions on the return on savings in an economy with annuities. Clearly, in an annuity market, the return on savings depends negatively on the proportion of survivors to the old age. Hence, the more individuals invest in their health, and the lower the return on annuities will be. This influence is obviously ignored by individuals, who may consider that each of them brings only a minor impact on the return.

But as all individuals buying annuities are in the same situation, the negative impact on savings return may be nonnegligible. To illustrate this, consider the following prevention choices under risk neutrality with respect to the duration of life. Individuals choose savings s and prevention H so as to maximize their expected lifetime well-being:

$$u(c) + \pi(H)u(d)$$

where $c = w - s - H$ and $d = sR/\pi(H)$. We assume a perfect annuity market, where the actuarially fair return $\tilde{R} = R/\pi(H)$ is decreasing in H. But in real life, individuals ignore the impact of H on $\tilde{R}$, and take $\tilde{R}$ as given. Hence, the FOC for prevention is, at the laissez-faire level:

$$u'(c) = \pi'(H)u(d)$$

whereas, at the social optimum, the FOC for optimal prevention would be:

$$u'(c) = \pi'(H)[u(d) - u'(d)d].$$

Taking into account the negative impact of prevention on the return on saving tends to reduce the marginal benefit from prevention, leading to a lower optimal prevention level in comparison with the laissez-faire level. Given that individuals neglect the impact of preventive spending on the return on savings, these tend to invest too much in their health in comparison with what would maximize their expected lifetime well-being. As a consequence, there is here an argument not for subsidizing, but for *taxing* prevention. This argument would be also valid in an economy without private annuities, but with a PAYG pension scheme. Here again, individuals spending into their health do not take into account its impact on pension benefits, which invites some taxation of prevention for the same reasons as the ones mentioned above. Note that the argument applies to fertility-enhancing decisions but in a reverse way. Instead of being taxed, those decisions should be subsidized. Consider the case in which individuals contribute to a PAYG pension and can choose their number of children. We posit $\pi = 1$ and $l = 1$ without loss of generality. Their problem amounts to maximizing:

$$u(c) - v(n) + u(d),$$

where $c = w - s - kn - \tau$ and $d = sR + p$. The number of children is given by n, k is the cost of raising a child, and p is the PAYG pension benefit. Assuming that all individuals are alike, we can write $p = \tau n$. Finally, $v(n)$ represents the utility of having n children. Here again we assume that individuals when choosing n take p as given and do not take into account the positive effect that fertility may have on the level of pensions. Thus the FOC for an individual utility maximization is different from that for a social welfare maximization. When choosing n, the individual is only concerned by its effect on $v(n)$. Namely:

$$u'(c)k = v'(n).$$

In contrast, social optimality implies:

$$u'(c)k = v'(n) + u'(d)\tau.$$

Going back to the issue of longevity, the argument remains valid once some degree of risk aversion with respect to the duration of life is introduced (through the transform $V(.)$). Indeed, in that case, the FOCs for optimal prevention is, at the laissez-faire level:

$$\pi'(H)\phi\left[u(c) + u\left(Rs/\pi(H)\right)\right] + \pi(H)\phi'\left[u(c) + u\left(Rs/\pi(H)\right)\right]\left[-u'(c)\right]$$
$$= \pi'(H)\phi\left[u(c)\right] + (1 - \pi(H))\phi'\left[u(c)\right]u'(c)$$

whereas the one for socially optimal prevention is:

$$\pi'(H)\phi\left[u(c) + u\left(Rs/\pi(H)\right)\right]$$
$$+ Rs/\pi(H\pi(H)\phi'\left[u(c) + u\left(Rs/\pi(H)\right)\right]\left[-u'(c) - u'(Rs/\pi(H)\frac{Rs\pi'(H)}{[\pi(H)]^2}\right]$$
$$= \pi'(H)\phi\left[u(c)\right] + (1 - \pi(H))\phi'\left[u(c)\right]u'(c).$$

Thus the tendency to overinvest in prevention also holds in this case. However, to the extent that risk aversion with respect to the duration of life

pushes towards more consumption early in life and reduces the amount of prevention, this may potentially reduce the size of the extent of overinvestment in
prevention.

5.4 Growth and Longevity

The simultaneous growth of economic activity and longevity observed during the last two centuries in industrialized countries has raised the issue of the
relationship between those two phenomena. In the recent years, the study of
interactions between economic development and longevity has been particularly enriched by OLG models with endogenous longevity (Chakraborty 2004;
Zhang et al. 2001, 2003; Pestieau et al. 2008). Here again the question is
whether the market solution leads to a social optimum and, if not, what kind of
feasible policy should be undertaken

Let us consider a two-period OLG model with identical individuals within
each generation (each generation being denoted by the time of its birth). Each
period of life is of a unit length. However, only a fraction π_{t+1} of a cohort born
at time t enjoys a second period of life ($0 < \pi_{t+1} < 1$). That proportion π_{t+1}
of survivors depends on health investments H_t made during the first period
of life. Formally, we have $\pi_{t+1} = \pi(H_t)$, where the function $\pi(H)$ can be
interpreted as a survival function. Whereas the first period is a period of work,
the second period is, for those who survive, a period of retirement. To avoid
accidental bequests, we introduce an annuity market with return R/π. If one
supposes that agents are expected-utility maximizers, and that life time welfare
is additive, the expected lifetime welfare of a member of generation t can be
written as:

$$U_t = \ln c_t + \pi(H_t) \ln d_{t+1}.$$

Health spending is assumed to be exclusively public and financed by a payroll tax τ_t, which implies that $x_t = \tau w_t$. This lifetime utility can be written in
explicit terms as:

$$U_t = \ln\left(w_t(1 - \tau_t) - s_t\right) + \pi(H_t) \ln\left(\frac{R_{t+1}}{\pi(H_t)} s_{t+1}\right).$$

Utility maximization implies a level of saving such that: $s_t = \sigma_t w_t (1 - \tau_t)$
where $\sigma_t = \pi_{t+1}/(1 - \pi_{t+1})$.

The production technology involves labor and capital and can be expressed
by the following Cobb-Douglas formulation: $F(K, L) = AK^\alpha L^{1-\alpha}$, or in inten-
sive terms

$$f(k) = Ak^\alpha.$$

From profit maximization, we obtain:

$$w_t = w(k_t) = Ak_t^\alpha; R_t = R(k_t) = A\alpha k_t^{\alpha-1}.$$

Given the equality between saving and capital accumulation, we obtain the key dynamic equation:

$$k_{t+1} = (1 - \tau)(1 - \alpha)\sigma(k_t)Ak_t^\alpha,$$

where

$$\sigma(k) = \frac{\pi(\tau(1 - \alpha)Ak^\alpha)}{1 + \pi(\tau(1 - \alpha)Ak^\alpha)}.$$

Depending on the parameters A, α, τ and on the function π, one can have different solutions for the growth path as well as for the steady state. The solutions range from one unique steady state that is stable to multiple steady states, some of them being unstable. If we take the case of a single stable steady state that is obtained for $\alpha < 1/2$, and two countries 1 and 2 just differing in their technology parameter A with $A_1 > A_2$, we have in the steady state $\hat{k}_1 > \hat{k}_2$ and the difference between those two levels of capital will the elasticity of π with respect to H. As Chakraborty (2004) puts it "endogeneous mortality induces a multiplier effect whereby differences in the technology parameter get amplified."

5.5 Longevity and Environment

It is widely acknowledged that natural environment constitutes a major determinant of longevity. Thus, it is not a surprise to find that life expectancy is strongly correlated across countries with environmental quality, as proxied by the Environmental Performance Index (see Section 2). This index takes into account both "environmental health" (as defined by drinking water, sanitation, pollution, etc.) and "ecosystem vitality", which includes factors such as biodiversity, availability of natural resources (forestry, fisheries, etc.), air quality, and energy. Therefore, reducing pollution or preserving natural resources may both contribute to improving environmental quality and to fostering longevity. At the same time, population increase induced by the increase of life expectancy has a negative effect on the environment for several reasons. Population size affects the total output level and thus the amount of pollution. Also, it generates an effect of congestion. It is thus worth modeling explicitly the two-way causality between environment and life expectancy.

In this setting, it is interesting to analyze the efficiency of the market and to study what a government, whose goal is to maximize social welfare in the long run, should do. We follow here the analysis of Jouvet et al. (2012). We thus use the standard two-period OLG economy, in which the length of the second period of life is influenced not only by private health expenditures, but also by environmental quality. Environmental quality enters this model in two distinct ways, each of these involving externalities, which can partially offset each other. First, the production process is assumed to generate polluting emissions, whose negative effects on longevity are not taken into account by producers. Second, environmental quality is assumed to influence welfare through the quantity of space available for each person. When choosing their health spending, individuals do not internalize the impact of their decisions on the number of persons. Note that these two external effects can partially, but not perfectly, offset one another. In this OLG model, agents of a cohort born at time t live a first period (of length 1), and enjoy a second period (of length $l_{t+1} < 1$). During young adulthood (i.e., period 1), each agent works, and gives birth to exactly one child. Then, at the old age (i.e., period 2), agents do not work, and consume their savings. The preferences of agents working in period t are represented by a standard time-additive utility function:

$$U_t = u(c_t, q_t) + l(H_t, P_{t+1})u(d_{t+1}, q_{t+1})$$

where c and d denote first and second period consumption, H is preventive health-care spending, P is the level of pollution, and $l_{t+1} = h(H_t, P_{t+1})$ represents the longevity function with $l_H > 0, l_{HH} < 0, l_P < 0, l_{PP} > 0$. Finally, we have:

$$q_t = \bar{Q}/N(1 + l(H_{t-1}, P_t))$$

where q_t is a measure of space per head at time t, $\bar{Q}$ being the total quantity of space and N the size of population. The utility function u(.,.) is supposed to be strictly quasi concave, with $u_i > 0$ (for $i = c, d$), $u_q > 0$ and $u_{iq} \geq 0$.

On the production side, one assumes the existence of a neoclassical production sector producing a single output Y_t by means of a quantity K_t of capital and a quantity L_t of labor. Capital fully depreciates during the process of production. The well-behaved production function is given by $Y_t = F(K_t, L)$. Profit maximization leads to $R_t = F_K(K_t, L_t)$ and $w_t = F_L(K_t, L_t)$. The flow of pollution emission, denoted by E_t, is equal to a proportion η of the current production, $E_t = \eta F(K_t, L_t)$ and the dynamics of the stock of pollution is given by the law $P_t = (1 - \delta)P_{t-1} + E_t$, where δ is the natural level of pollution absorption ($0 \leq \delta \leq 1$).

To obtain the social optimum conditions, one finds the values of c, H, and k that maximize U in the steady state subject to the constraint:

$$f(k) = c + x + dl(H, P) + k,$$

where $f(k)$ and k are per capita output and capital. From the FOCs, we obtain:

$$u_c' = u_d$$

$$u_c (1 + l_H d) = l_H \left[u(c, q) - \frac{q\mu}{(1 + l)} \right] \tag{21}$$

$$f'(k) = 1 - f'(k) lu \frac{\eta}{\delta} N \left[\frac{u(d, q) - d u_d}{u_d} - \frac{q\mu}{(1 + l) u_d} \right] \tag{22}$$

where $\mu = u_q(c, q) + l u_q(d, q)$ is the marginal utility of q over the lifetime. Note that the last two conditions would simplify to:

$$u_c(c, q) (1 + l_H d) = l_H u(c, q); f'(k) = 1,$$

in the case there would be no pollution or congestion. The congestion term $q\mu/(1 + l)$ is a cost (alternatively a negative benefit) that has to be added to the cost of health care.

With the environmental variables, we have some externalities. As stated above, the externality associated to the health investment decision (eq. (21)) comes from the fact that individuals do not internalize, in their decisions, the effect of increased longevity on the space available for each. The choice of investment (eq. (22)) entails two distinct externalities. The first externality is a negative one: more pollution means lower longevity, and, thus, a lower utility in the second period of life ceteris paribus. The second externality is a positive one: more capital means more pollution, and, thus, a lower population pressure, which is good for the quality of the environment. Substituting (21) into (22), one can show that the negative externality dominates the positive one. This implies that the optimum level of capital accumulation should be lower than that corresponding to the standard golden rule level.

In the same line, Raffin and Seegmuller (2014) analyze the interplay between longevity, pollution, and growth within an OLG model, where longevity, pollution and growth are endogenous. The authorities may provide two types of public service, public health and environmental maintenance, that participate to extend agents' life expectancy and to sustain growth in the long term. They show that global dynamics might be featured by a high growth rate equilibrium, associated with longer life expectancy and an environmental poverty trap. They examine changes in public policies: increasing public intervention on health or environmental maintenance display opposite effects on global dynamics, i.e., on the size of the trap and on the level of the stable balanced growth path.

5.6 Optimal Lockdown Policy in the case of a Pandemic

According to the journal *Nature*,[9] 3.2 million people would have died during the first wave of the COVID-19 pandemic (more precisely from the start of the pandemic to May 4, 2020) if not for measures such as closing businesses and telling people to stay at home. To take the specific example of France, lockdown saved around 690,000 lives as opposed to the actual loss of about 30,000 lives during the same period. At the same time, French GDP dropped at the fastest rate in history, contracting 14 percent in the second quarter, and the rate of unemployment exploded. Those figures show quite clearly that, in times of pandemic, there is a trade-off between economic prosperity and saving human lives. The way this trade-off is solved reflects the weight governments puts on those two dimensions. On that basis, the French government preferred to save 690,000 lives at the expenses of a loss of 14 percent of national income. This brings us to the question of the optimal lockdown policy that requires to assess the gains and losses from maintaining the economy under more or less strong sanitary constraints. This question is dealt with in Pestieau and Ponthière (2022). Deriving an optimal lockdown policy requires that one first agrees on a social objective that should incorporate and weight all aspects of individual interests in the population under study. Following the discussion in Section 3, we examine the solution of the optimal lockdown problem under two social welfare criteria: the utilitarian and the ex post egalitarian social criterion, which gives absolute priority to the worst off ex post. Let us consider a simple model of the human life cycle in the presence of an epidemic. There are two ages of life – the young age and the old age – and the duration of each period of life is normalized to unity. Young individuals are active, while old individuals are retired. The number of young adults is denoted by $N > 0$. An epidemic takes place in the society, and increases the strength of mortality. Let us denote by $\pi(Z, I)$ the probability to enjoy old age. Abstracting from infant and childhood mortality, life expectancy at birth in our economy is thus equal to $1 + \pi$. The probability of survival to the old age is assumed to be decreasing with the degree of prevalence of the epidemic, denoted by I, and to be increasing with the strength of the lockdown policy chosen by the government, denoted by Z. Both I and Z take values in the interval $(0, 1)$.

National production is given by $Y = Y(N, Z)$ where $Y_N > 0$, $Y_{NN} < 0$ and $Y_Z < 0$, where N is the size of the labor force. We assume that the retirees benefit from a defined benefit PAYG pension, the pension benefit being b. We denote first period consumption by c. Both population growth rate and interest

---

[9] Flaxman et al. (2020).

rates are nil. There is no saving. The lifetime expected utility of an individual is given by:

$$EU = Nu(c) + \pi(Z, I))u(b)$$

where:

$$c = \frac{Y(N, Z) - \pi(Z, I))Nb}{N}.$$

5.6.1 Utilitarian Criterion

In this simple presentation, we implicitly assume that we are in a steady state situation such that the welfare of the retired in a given of period of time is also the welfare that an individual can expect to enjoy when retired. Thus the maximization of the expected utility is equivalent to the maximization of a utilitarian social welfare expressed as:

$$SW^U = N[u(c) + \pi(Z, I))u(b)].$$

The two instruments are Z and b.

The FOCs are:

$$u'(c) = u'(b)$$

and

$$\frac{\partial SW^U}{\partial Z} = u'(c)[Y_Z(N, Z)/N - \pi_Z(Z, I)b] + \pi_Z(Z, I)u(b). \qquad (23)$$

The first FOC is standard; it implies smoothing of consumption. The second condition says that the cost of a lockdown policy should be equal to its benefit. There is a double cost in this specification: increasing Z reduces the level of output Y and it increases social spending because of the defined benefit assumption. Equation (23) can be rewritten as:

$$\frac{\partial SW^U}{\partial Z} = Y_Z(N, Z)/N + \pi_Z(Z, I)\left[\frac{u(b)}{u'(b)} - b\right].$$

The ratio $\frac{u(b)}{u'(b)}$ is the coefficient of fear of ruin that is related to standard measures of risk aversion. As $u(b)$ is concave, one has that $\frac{u(b)}{u'(b)} - b$ is nonnegative and increases with risk aversion.

In the case where there is no pandemic, $I = 0$ and $Z = 0$. With $I > 0$, lockdown becomes desirable if $\frac{\partial SW^U}{\partial Z}\big|_{Z=0} > 0$. A sufficient condition would be that $\varphi_Z(0, I) = \infty$. If the effect of lockdown on economic activity is weak, one can have that the optimal policy is $Z = 1$. This corresponds to the highest level of population and is related to the well-known repugnant solution. In a seminal work, Parfit (1984) showed that classical utilitarianism suffers, under mild conditions, from the repugnant conclusion, in the sense that for any large population of individuals having a low utility level, it is always possible to find another, even larger, population, where each individual enjoys an even lower welfare level, but such that total welfare is larger.

5.6.2 Ex Post Egalitarianism

In our simple model where everyone is identical ex ante, there are two types of individual ex post: the short- and the long-lived. Without lockdown ($Z = 0$) and with $I = 0$, the lifetime utilities of the short-lived and the long-lived would be:

$$U_S = u(\frac{Y(N,0)}{N} - \pi\,(0,0)\,b)$$

$$U_L = u(\frac{Y(N,0)}{N} - \pi\,(0,0)\,b) + u(b).$$

We then observe welfare inequalities due to unequal lifetimes. These are a matter of pure luck, and one may argue that such arbitrary welfare inequalities should be abolished by the government. One way to advocate for such an abolishment of welfare inequalities due to circumstances consists of referring to the Principle of Compensation (see Fleurbaey & Maniquet 2004; Fleurbaey 2008). According to the Principle of Compensation, welfare inequalities due to circumstances should be abolished. In this particular case, ex post equality can be established granted that $b = \bar{c}$ where $u(\bar{c}) = 0$.

We now assume that $I > 0$ and look for the optimal lockdown policy. The ex post utilities are the following:

$$U_S = u(\frac{Y(N,Z)}{N} - \pi\,(Z,I)\,b)$$

$$U_L = u(\frac{Y(N,Z)}{N} - \pi\,(Z,I)\,b) + u(b).$$

It can be immediately established that the optimal ex post policy is $Z = 0$ and $b = \bar{c}$. This is intuitive: such policy equates the two utilities and grant the highest first period consumption possible:

$$U_S = U_L = u(\frac{Y(N,0)}{N} - \pi\,(0,I)\,b).$$

5.7 Fear of Ruin and Rectangularization

In Section 5.2, we dealt with the trade-off between preventive and curative longevity enhancing investment focusing on the possible myopic attitudes that some individuals may exhibit towards the beneficial effect of prevention. We now see how this trade-off can impact the rectangularization of the survival.[10] We use our standard model with two parameters: one representing the limit of a human lifespan and one representing the probability of reaching that age limit after a certain age. If this probability increases, we get an increasingly rectangular survival curve. If, instead, the age limit increases, we have a parallel shift of the survival curve. The distinction between those two ways of increasing longevity raises interesting normative problems. In this section, we want to show that under reasonable assumptions about the utility function and the technology, risk-averse decision makers will tend to favor the increase in the survival probability (and hence rectangularization). In this framework, risk aversion is measured through the concept of "fear of ruin," which was first proposed by Aumann and Kurz (1977) and was analyzed in depth by Foncel and Treich (2005).

Each individual is thus assumed to live for sure during the first period, which has a length time normalized to 1. They face at the beginning of the second period a probability of death denoted π. If they survive they will live for a time length denoted l with $l \leq 1$. Both π and l can be influenced by choices made at the beginning of the first period. We denote by x efforts that are undertaken to increase π and e are efforts chosen ex ante to increase l. Both functions $\pi(x)$ and $l(e)$ are strictly concave. Besides the investment choices x and e made at the beginning of the first period, the individual has also to decide on their saving level s. Given earnings available at the beginning of the first period and denoted w, current consumption of the first period c is expressed as:

$$c = w - s - x - e.$$

In the second period, consumption level d is determined by the rate of return of the savings that had been invested in an annuity market, which is more or less fair. The rate of return of this annuity is given by $R = \frac{1+r}{(\pi h)^\alpha}$, where r is the rate of interest and $\alpha \in (0, 1)$ reflects the fairness of the annuity. With $\alpha = 0$, there is no annuity and with $\alpha = 1$, the annuity is actuarially fair. The utility function of the decision maker in each period (u) has two arguments: consumption and length of life. The intertemporal expected utility U is then given by:

$$U = u(w - s - x - e, 1) + \pi (x) u(sR, l(e)). \tag{24}$$

If the individual dies at the beginning of the second period, the current utility is equal to zero (because there is no bequest motive). Then, by symmetry, when $l(e)$ tends to zero, $u(sR, l(e))$ also tends to zero so that necessarily $u(d, 0) = 0$.

---

[10] This section draws on Eeckhoudt and Pestieau (2008).

We assume that each first derivative of u is strictly positive while each direct second derivative is nonpositive.

The first-order conditions with respect to s, x, and e associated to the objective function defined in (24) are given by:

$$u_1(c, 1) = \pi(x)Ru_1(d, l(e))$$

$$u_1(c, 1) = \pi'(x)u(d, l(e)) \tag{25}$$

$$u_1(c, 1) = \pi(x)l'(e)u_2(d, l(e)). \tag{26}$$

Since we are going to focus exclusively on the link between x and e, we take s as given. Comparison of equations (25) and (26) yields:

$$\frac{\pi'(x)}{\pi(x)} = \frac{l'(e)}{l(e)} \cdot \frac{u_2(d, l(e))l(e)}{u(d, l(e))}.$$

Hence, we obtain:

$$\frac{\pi'(x)}{\pi(x)} \lessgtr \frac{l'(e)}{l(e)} \Leftrightarrow \frac{u_2(d, l(e))l(e)}{u(d, l(e))} \lessgtr 1.$$

The term $\frac{u_2(d,l(e))}{u(d,l(e))}$ is the inverse of the "fear of ruin" (denoted FR) with respect to $l(e)$, the length of life. As shown by Foncel and Treich (2005), FR is an index of risk aversion. When the utility function is concave in $l(e)$ and when $u(d, 0) = 0$ (for reasons indicated before), it is easily shown that $\frac{u_2 l}{u} < 1$.

As a result, when the decision maker becomes risk averse with respect to lotteries on survival time, one has:

$$\frac{\pi'(x)}{\pi(x)} < \frac{l'(e)}{l(e)} \tag{27}$$

and because of the assumption made about the survival technology, this implies inside a budget constraint that x^* increases and e^* falls.

Note that if had chosen a utility function reflecting risk neutrality with respect to lotteries on survival time, we would have $u(d, l(e)) = u(d)l(e)$. This implies that the individual cares only about expected survival and that, at the optimum,

$$\frac{\pi'(x)}{\pi(x)} = \frac{l'(e)}{l(e)}.$$

To conclude, with inequality (27), individuals prefer to increase their longevity in the direction of rectangularization of their survival curve instead of an upward shift of the curve. The two types of effort, x and e, do not affect the variance of survival length πl in the same way. It is nonmonotonic in π, reaching a maximum at $\pi = 1/2$. In contrast, this variance is an increasing and convex function of *e*. As a consequence, risk averse individuals will systematically prefer increases in x relative to increases in y. Note that this result is related to Bommier (2006) and his rejection of traditional lifecycle models. As seen in Section 3, these models imply risk neutrality with respect to longevity.

6 Conclusion

Our societies are witnessing a steady increase in longevity. This evolution is accompanied by some convergence across countries but a rather stable dispersion among individuals. Longevity differences between men and women, skilled and unskilled workers, nationals and immigrants are important and sometimes increasing. To a large extent public policies are ill adapted to this reality. One can indeed question to what extent the observed lengthening of life makes existing policies obsolete and inadequate. The purpose of this Element is to survey the implications that changing longevity may have on the design of optimal public policy.

For that purpose, we started by considering empirical facts, and noted that the observed rise in life expectancy should not hide the risky nature of life and the resulting longevity inequalities. Then, we developed a simple theoretical framework, which helped us to discuss some major challenges raised by increasing life expectancy. We first examined the representation of individual preferences, and underlined the difficulty to account for risk aversion with respect to the length of life. Then, we considered the choice of a social welfare criterion, and highlighted the limits of the utilitarian and of the ex ante approaches, and studied the roles of responsibility and luck.

With these foundations, we turned to the impact of changes in longevity on various public policies in two sections. The fourth section considered the case of exogenous longevity. With this assumption, we analyzed the impact of differential mortality rates on the design of public pensions, the effect of aging on the structure and distribution of wealth, the incidence of longevity increases on education and growth, the interaction between aging and pension systems on growth, the role of income differentiated mortality on poverty alleviation, on the taxation of inheritance and on the combined choice of public pension and public LTC insurance. In the fifth section, we assumed endogenous longevity. Within this setting, we studied a number of issues: the optimal taxation or subsidy of capital income and health spending, the choice of preventive versus curative investment, the externality that longevity enhancing behavior can have on annuities, and the optimal lockdown in case of a pandemic.

Although the Element does not have the pretension to completeness, it suggests, nonetheless, that longevity changes invite a deep adaptation of economic fundamentals, on both a positive side (preferences) and a normative side (social welfare criterion). Given that varying longevity also raises serious policy issues in terms of pensions, social insurance, health care and long-term care, it is not an exaggeration to conclude that, inspite of the voluminous literature surveyed here, a lot of work remains to be done to take longevity seriously, that is, to reconsider the numerous policy issues discussed here in the light of more adequate economic fundamentals (individual and social preferences). Longevity changes will thus remain, for some time to come, a key challenge for economists.

References

Arias, E. (2014): United States life tables, 2009, National Vital Statistics Reports, vol. 62 no. 7, Hyattsville, MD, National Center for Health Statistics.

Atkinson, A. & J. Stiglitz (1976): The design of tax structure: direct versus indirect taxation, *Journal of Public Economics*, 6 (1–2), 55–75.

Atkinson A. & J. Stiglitz (1980): *Lectures on public economics*, New York, McGraw-Hill.

Aumann, R. & M. Kurz (1977): Power and taxes, *Econometrica*, 45, 1137–63.

Balia, S. & A. Jones (2008): Mortality, lifestyle and socioeconomic status, *Journal of Health Economics*, 27 (1), 1–26.

Baurin, A. (2020): The limited power of socioeconomic status to predict longevity: implications for pension policy, LIDAM Discussion Papers IRES 2020019.

Becker, G. & T. Philipson (1998): Old age longevity and mortality contingent claims, *Journal of Political Economy*, 106, 551–73.

Ben-Porath, Y. (1967): The production of human capital and the life-cycle of earnings, *Journal of Political Economy*, 75, 352–65.

Bentham, J. (1789): An introduction to the principles of morals and legislation, London.

Bernoulli, D. (1730): Specimen theoriae novae de mensura sortis (English translation: Exposition of a new theory on the measurement of risk), *Econometrica*, 22, 23–36.

Blackburn, K. & G. Cipriani (2002): A model of longevity, fertility and growth, *Journal of Economic Dynamics and Control*, 26, 187–204.

Bloom, D., D. Canning, & M. Moore (2007): A theory of retirement, NBER Working Papers 13630.

Bommier, A. (2006): Uncertain lifetime and intertemporal choice: risk aversion as a rationale for time discounting, *International Economic Review*, 47 (4), 1223–46.

Bommier, A. (2007): Risk aversion, intertemporal elasticity of substitution and correlation aversion, *Economics Bulletin*, 29, 1–8.

Bommier, A. (2010): Portfolio choice under uncertain lifetime, *Journal of Public Economic Theory*, 12 (1), 57–73.

Boucekkine, R., B. Diene, & T. Azomahou (2008): Growth economics of epidemics: a review of the theory, *Mathematical Population Studies*, 15 (1), 1–26.

Broome, J. (2004): Weighing lives, New York, Oxford University Press.

Case, A. & A. Deaton (2020): Deaths of despair and the future of capitalism, Princeton University Press.

Chakraborty, S. (2004): Endogenous lifetime and economic growth, *Journal of Economic Theory*, 116, 119–37.

Christensen, K., T. Johnson, & J. Vaupel (2006): The quest for genetic determinants of human longevity: challenges and insights, *Nature Reviews - Genetics*, 7, 436–48.

Contoyannis, P. & Jones, A. (2004): Socio-economic status, health and lifestyle, *Journal of Health Economics*, 23, 965–95.

Cremer, H., P. Dedonder, D. Maldonado, & P. Pestieau (2012): Taxing sin goods and subsidizing health care, *Scandinavian Journal of Economics*, forthcoming.

Dedry, A., H. Onder, & P. Pestieau (2018): Aging, social security design and capital accumulation, *Journal of the Economics of Aging*, 9, 145–55.

de la Croix, D. & O. Licandro (1999): Life expectancy and endogenous growth, *Economics Letters*, 65, 255–63.

de la Croix, D. & O. Licandro (2012): The child is the father of the man: implications for the demographic transition, *Economic Journal*, 123, 236–61.

Diamond, P. & J. Spinnewijn (2011): Capital income taxes with heterogeneous discount rates, *American Economic Journal: Economic Policy*, 3 (4), 52–76.

Eeckhoudt, L. & P. Pestieau (2008): Fear of ruin and longevity enhancing investment, *Economics Letters*, 101, 57–9.

Ehrlich, I. & F. Lui (1991): Intergenerational trace, longevity and economic growth, *Journal of Political Economy*, 1029–60.

Flaxman, S. et al. (2020): Estimating the effects of non-pharmaceutical interventions on COVID-19 in Europe, *Nature*, 584, 257–61.

Fleurbaey, M. (2008): Fairness, responsibility and welfare, New York, Oxford University Press.

Fleurbaey, M., M.-L. Leroux, & G. Ponthière, (2014): Compensating the dead, *Journal of Mathematical Economics*, 51, 28–41.

Fleurbaey, M. & F. Maniquet (2004): Compensation and responsibility, in K. Arrow, A. Sen, & K. Suzumura (eds.), Handbook of social choice and welfare, vol 2., Amsterdam, North-Holland.

Foncel, J. & N. Treich (2005): Fear of ruin, *Journal of Risk and Uncertainty*, 31, 289–300.

Fong, G., D. Hammond, F. Laux, M. Zanna, M. Cummings, R. Borland, & R. Hana (2004): The near experience of regret among smokers in four countries: findings from the International Tobacco Control Policy Evaluation Survey, *Nicotine and Tobacco Research*, 6, S341–S351.

Heijdra, B. & J. Mierau (2011): The individual life cycle and economic growth: an essay on demographic macroeconomics, The *De Economist*, 159, 63–87.

Hendi, A. (2017): Trends in education-specific life expectancy, data quality and shifting education distributions: a note on recent research, *Demography*, 54, 1203–13.

Human Mortality Database (2012): University of California, Berkeley (USA), Max Planck Institute for Demographic Research (Germany), available at www.mortality.org. Data downloaded on August 2012.

Ito, H. & K. Tabata (2008): Demographic structure and growth: the effect of unfunded social security, *Economics Letters*, 100, 288–91.

Jarvis, M., D. McIntyre, & Clive Bates (2002): Effectiveness of smoking cessation initiatives, *British Medical Journal*, 324, 608.

Jouvet, P.-A., P. Pestieau, & G. Ponthière (2010): Longevity and environmental quality in an OLG model, *Journal of Economics*, 100, 191–216.

Kalemli-Ozcan, S., H. Ryder, & David Weil (2000): Mortality decline, human capital investment, and economic growth, *Journal of Development Economics*, 62, 1–23.

Kaplan, G., T. Seeman, R. Cohen, L. Knudsen, & J. Guralnik (1987): Mortality among the elderly in the Almeda county study: behavioral and demographic risk factors, *American Journal of Public Health*, 77, 307–12.

Klimaviciute, J., P. Pestieau, & H. Onder (2019): Inherited wealth and demographic aging, *German Economic Review*, 20, 4 , 872–91.

Kremer, M. (1993) Population growth and technological change: one billion B.C. to 1990, *Quarterly Journal of Economics*, 108, 681–716.

Lefèbvre M., S. Perelman, & J. Schoenmaeckers (2018): Inégalités face à la mort et au risque de dépendance, *Revue Française d'Economie*, 33, 75–112.

Lefèbvre, M., P. Pestieau, & G. Ponthière (2018): FGT poverty measures and the mortality paradox. Theory and evidence, *Review of Income and Wealth*, 64, 428–58.

Lefèbvre, M., P. Pestieau, & G. Ponthière (2019a): Premature mortality and poverty measurement in an OLG economy, *Journal of Population Economics*, 32, 621–64.

Lefèbvre, M., P. Pestieau & G. Ponthière (2019b): Missing poor and income mobility, *Journal of Comparative Economics*, 47, 330–66.

Leker, L. & G. Ponthière (2015): Education, life expectancy and family bargaining: the Ben-Porath effect revisited, *Education Economics*, 23, 481–513.

Leroux, M.-L., P. Pestieau, & G. Ponthière (2011a): Longevity, genes and effort: an optimal taxation approach to prevention, *Journal of Health Economics*, 30 (1), 62–75.

Leroux, M.-L., P. Pestieau, & G. Ponthière (2011b): Optimal linear taxation under endogenous longevity, *Journal of Population Economics*, 24 (1), 213–37.

Leroux, M.-L. & G. Ponthière (2009): Optimal tax policy and expected longevity: a mean-variance utility approach, *International Tax and Public Finance*, 16, 514–37.

Leroux, M.-L. & P. Pestieau (2021): Age and health related inheritance taxation, CORE DP 2021/02.

Lutz, W., G. Amran, & A. Belanger (2019): Demographic scenarios for the EU–migration, population and education, Brussels, publications Office of the European Union.

Marois, G., A. Bélanger, & W. Lutz (2020): Population aging, migration, and productivity in Europe, www.researchgate.net/publication/340105385_Population_aging_migration_and_productivity_in_Europe

Miyazawa, K. (2006): Growth and inequality: a demographic explanation, *Journal of Population Economics*, 19, 559–78.

Newman, S. (2019): Supercentenarians and the oldest-old are concentrated into regions with no birth certificates and short lifespans, Researchgate.

Nishimura Y. & P. Pestieau (2016): Efficient taxation with differential risks of dependence and mortality, *Economics Bulletin*, 36 (1), 52–7.

Nishimura, Y., P. Pestieau, & G. Ponthière (2018): Education choices, longevity and optimal policy in a Ben-Porath economy, *Journal of Mathematical Social Sciences*, 94, 65–81.

Nishimura, Y. & P. Pestieau (2021): Old age or dependence. Which social insurance? Unpublished.

Nusselder, W. & J. Mackenbach (2000): Lack of improvement of life expectancy at advanced ages in the Netherlands, *International Journal of Epidemiology*, 29, 140–8.

OECD (2018): The role and design of net wealth taxes in the OECD, OECD Tax Policy Studies, Paris, OECD.

OECD (2020): Ageing and employment policies – statistics on average effective age of retirement, Paris, OECD.

Parfit, D. (1984): Reasons and persons, New York, Oxford University Press.

Pestieau, P. & G. Ponthière (2014a): On the policy implications of changing longevity, *CESifo Economic Studies*, 60, 178–213.

Pestieau, P. & G. Ponthière (2014b): Longevity variations and the welfare state, *Journal of Demographic Economy*, 82, 216–39.

Pestieau, P. & M. Racionero Llorente (2016): Harsh occupations, life expectancy and social security, *Economic Modelling*, 58, 194–202.

Pestieau, P., G. Ponthière, & M. Sato (2008): Longevity, health spendings and PAYG pensions, FinanzArchiv – Public Finance Analysis, 64 (1), 1–18.

Pestieau, P. & G. Ponthière (2022): Optimal lockdown and social welfare. Journal of Population Economics, 35:241–268.

Piketty, T. & E. Saez (2013): A theory of optimal inheritance taxation, *Econometrica*, 81 (5), 1851–86.

Raffin, N. & T. Seegmuller (2014): Longevity, pollution and growth, *Mathematical Social Sciences*, 69, 22–33.

Rawls, J. (1971): A theory of justice, Cambridge, MA: Harvard University Press.

Rochet, J.-C. (1991): Incentives, redistribution and social insurance, *Geneva Risk and Insurance Review*, 16 (2), 143–65.

Samuelson, P. (1975): The optimum growth rate for population, *International Economic Review*, 16, 531–8.

Sen, A. K. (1998): Mortality as an indicator of economic success and failure, *Economic Journal*, 108, 1–25.

Slovic, P. (2001): Cigarette smokers: rational actors or rational fools?, in P. Slovic (ed.), Smoking: risk, perception, and policy, pp. 97–126, Thousand Oaks, CA: Sage.

Tabata, K. (2014): Population aging and growth: the effect of PAYG pension reform. Unpublished.

Teixeira, L., L. Araujo, C. Paul, & O. Ribeiro (2020): Centenarians. A European overview, Springer Briefs in Aging, Springer.

United Nations (2001): Replacement migration: is it a solution to declining and ageing populations? New York, United Nations, Department of Economic and Social Affairs, Population Division.

Vickrey, W. (1945): An integrated successions tax. Republished in R. Arnott, K. Arrow, A. Atkinson, & J. Dreze (eds.) (1994): Public economics. Selected papers by William Vickrey, Cambridge University Press.

Wendling, Z., A. Sherbinin, J. Emerson, & D. Esty (2020) Environmental performance index, Yale Center for Environmental Law and Policy.

Yaari, M. (1965): Uncertain lifetime, life insurance and the theory of the consumer, *Review of Economic Studies*, 32, 137–50.

Zhang, J., J. Zhang, & R. Lee (2001): Mortality decline and long-run economic growth, *Journal of Public Economics*, 80, 485–507.

Zhang, J., J. Zhang, & R. Lee (2003): Rising longevity, education, savings and growth, *Journal of Development Economics*, 70, 83–101.

Acknowledgments

Financial support from the Chaire "Marché des risques et création de valeur" of the FdR/SCOR is gratefully acknowledged.

Cambridge Elements ≡

Public Economics

Robin Boadway
Queen's University

Robin Boadway is Emeritus Professor of Economics at Queen's University. His main research interests are in public economics, welfare economics and fiscal federalism.

Frank A. Cowell
London School of Economics and Political Science

Frank A. Cowell is Professor of Economics at the London School of Economics. His main research interests are in inequality, mobility and the distribution of income and wealth.

Massimo Florio
University of Milan

Massimo Florio is Professor of Public Economics at the University of Milan. His main interests are in cost-benefit analysis, regional policy, privatization, public enterprise, network industries and the socio-economic impact of research infrastructures.

About the Series

The Cambridge Elements of Public Economics provides authoritative and up-to-date reviews of core topics and recent developments in the field. It includes state-of-the-art contributions on all areas in the field. The editors are particularly interested in the new frontiers of quantitative methods in public economics, experimental approaches, behavioral public finance, empirical and theoretical analysis of the quality of government and institutions.

Cambridge Elements ≡

Public Economics

Elements in the Series

A full series listing is available at: www.cambridge.org/ElePubEcon

Printed in the United States
by Baker & Taylor Publisher Services